INTRODUCTION

The goal of **EXPLORATIONS IN MUSIC, Books 1-7** is to expand the idea of music theory to points beyond the written page, to have your students realize that the music they are performing, listening to, and composing evolves from the realm of music theory.

I believe students can best understand how music is constructed by working with each musical idea in a number of different ways—writing, listening, analyzing scores, investigating their own repertoire, experimenting with composing, and various other creative activities. With this broad understanding, your students will make connections between the study of music theory and the music they hear, perform, and create.

Joanne Haroutounian
Arlington, Virginia

FEATURES OF EXPLORATIONS IN MUSIC, Books 1-7

- **Students explore and discover** new concepts.

- **Each concept** is used in a variety of ways, always including opportunities for creativity.

- **Creative experimentation** encourages students to compose.

- **Listening** examples are interwoven throughout the book and presented on a cassette tape. Students make the "eye and ear" connections with the score.

- **Cassette tapes** are provided with each book to allow listening to be done outside of lesson time—at home or in theory classes.

- **Explore** sections allow students to analyze the musical score with "eye and ear"and work creatively with musical ideas.

- **Explore Bonus** sections offer the curious student a challenge, providing motivation to work beyond what is already presented.

- **Beyond the Page** sections offer opportunities to link the student's current repertoire directly to the concepts developed in **EXPLORATIONS IN MUSIC.**

- A **Teacher's Guide** is correlated to each student book, providing many extra creative activities and the answers.

JOANNE HAROUTOUNIAN

Joanne Haroutounian has several special interests in music. She teaches piano students in her Arlington, Virginia, studio and engages them in many creative studio projects. She is also on the adjunct faculty of George Mason University. She has taught general music in the public schools and music education at the college level.

Joanne frequently performs chamber music with her husband, William, a violinist with the National Symphony. Her explorations into the area of arts education for gifted students led her to pursue a doctorate in educational psychology/gifted education at the University of Virginia.

She has presented numerous workshops on piano pedagogy, chamber music, special studio projects, and gifted education at local and state conventions as well as at the Music Teachers National Association, National Association for Gifted Children, and the National Conference on Piano Pedagogy.

Other publications by Mrs. Haroutounian are *Rhythm Antics* for elementary musicians, *Hummel's Concertino for Piano, op. 73* (two-piano score), and *Chamber Music Sampler Book* for piano, violin, and cello. All books are published by the Neil A. Kjos Music

D1383603

VP350

WHAT WILL YOU DO?

 **WRITE**   Apply each new idea you learn through writing.

 **ANALYZE**   Discover details in the music by analyzing with your eyes and ears.

 **LISTEN**   Listen to the cassette tape to recognize new information in performed music and to develop skills through ear-training exercises. Each listening example is numbered in the book and announced on the tape.

 **INVESTIGATE**   Search for new ideas in this book and in the music you perform to discover specific information.

 **CREATE**   Experiment with your ideas by composing. Use your imagination to stretch your mind and your senses.

 **EXPLORE**   Learn to be curious! Research and expand on musical ideas.

Joanne Haroutounian

EXPLORATIONS IN MUSIC

BOOK 1 CONTENTS

The **EXPLORATIONS IN MUSIC, Book 1** cassette includes listening examples for each time you see the symbol ♫.
The compilation of the following excerpts is provided by PolyGram Special Markets, a division of Polygram Group Distribution, Inc. ℗ 1993:
Jean-Philippe Rameau: *Gavotte et Doubles from Nouvelles Suites de Pieces de Clavecin,* Christophe Rousset, Harpsichord
Wolfgang Amadeus Mozart: *German Dance K.605 No. 2,* Wiener Mozart-Ensemble, Willi Boskovsky, Conductor
Joseph Haydn: *Menuet e Trio from Symphony No. 48 in C Major ("Maria Theresia")* Philharmonia Hungarica, Antal Dorati, Conductor
Antonio Vivaldi: *Allegro from Concerto No. 3 in D, RV 428 ("Il gardellino"),* I Musici, Severino Gazzelloni, Flute

| WP350 | ISBN 0-8497-9531-1 | book and cassette |
| WP350B | ISBN 0-8497-9562-1 | book only |

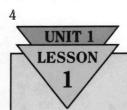

UNIT 1
LESSON 1

THE STAFF: LINES AND SPACES

Music is written on a music **STAFF**. The staff is made up of **LINES** and **SPACES**.

LINES

1. Count the number of **lines** you see on the staff above. There are _____ lines.

   The notes below are written on the **lines** of the staff. A line goes through the **middle** of each note.

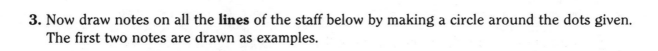

2. Draw notes on the single line below. Remember, **the line goes through the middle of each note.**

3. Now draw notes on all the **lines** of the staff below by making a circle around the dots given. The first two notes are drawn as examples.

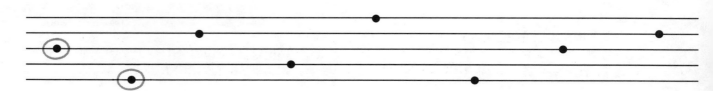

4. Notes written correctly on the **lines** of the staff **have the line going exactly through the middle of the note.** Draw an **X** on all the line notes that are drawn **incorrectly** on the staff below.

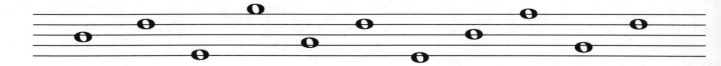

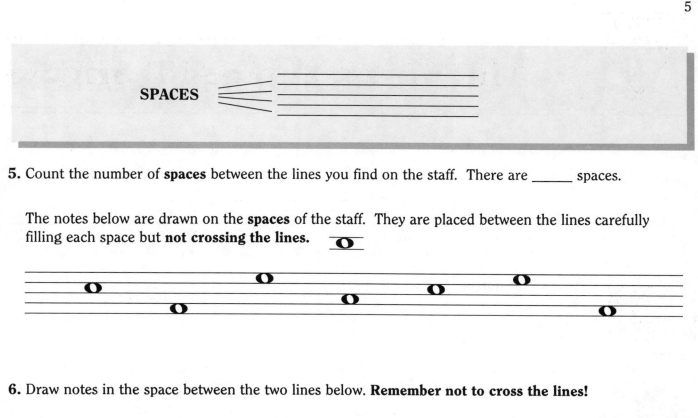

SPACES

5. Count the number of **spaces** between the lines you find on the staff. There are _____ spaces.

The notes below are drawn on the **spaces** of the staff. They are placed between the lines carefully filling each space but **not crossing the lines.**

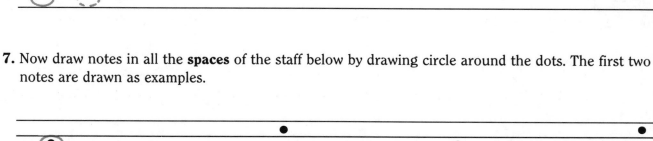

6. Draw notes in the space between the two lines below. **Remember not to cross the lines!**

7. Now draw notes in all the **spaces** of the staff below by drawing circle around the dots. The first two notes are drawn as examples.

8. Notes drawn correctly on the **spaces** of the staff **fill the space without crossing the lines.** Draw an **X** on all the space notes drawn **incorrectly** on the staff below.

EXPLORE Have fun with your imagination! Draw something that will remind you of notes written on a **line** or **space.**

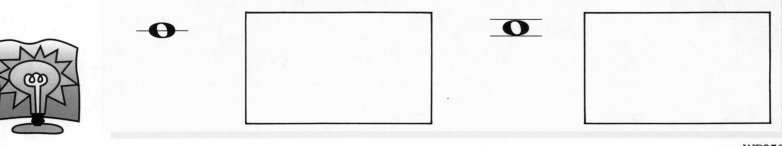

LINE NOTE	YOUR PICTURE	SPACE NOTE	YOUR PICTURE

TREBLE AND BASS CLEFS

The **TREBLE CLEF** is written on the staff that shows notes that are **HIGH** in pitch.
The bracket over the piano keyboard below shows the keys that have notes written in the **TREBLE STAFF.**

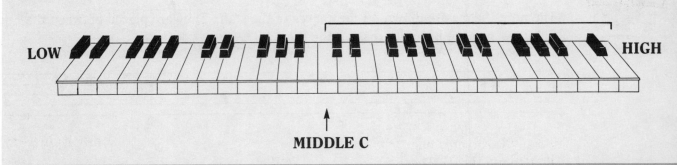

LOW   HIGH

↑
MIDDLE C

1. The **treble clef** is drawn around the **second line up from the BOTTOM of the staff**. Follow the steps below, tracing the dotted lines and drawing **treble clefs.**

1.	2.	3.	TRACE	YOUR TURN

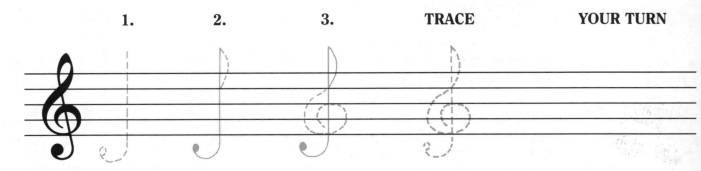

The **BASS CLEF** is drawn on the staff that shows notes that are **LOW** in pitch.
The bracket over the piano keyboard below shows the keys that have notes written in the **BASS STAFF.**

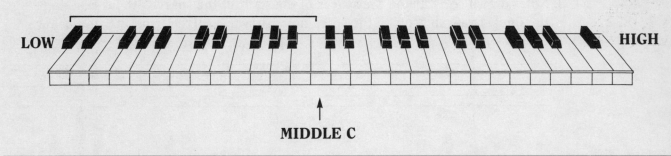

LOW   HIGH

↑
MIDDLE C

2. The **bass clef** is drawn around **the second line from the TOP of the staff**. Follow the steps below, tracing the lines and drawing **bass clefs.**

1.	2.	3.	TRACE	YOUR TURN

EXPLORE

The notes written in the **TREBLE STAFF** and the **BASS STAFF** describe sounds of many instruments as well as sounds we sing. Keyboard instruments such as the piano, organ, or synthesizer use the treble staff and bass staff together to make a **GRAND STAFF:**

Some instruments play only notes that sound **HIGH**. These instruments use the **TREBLE STAFF** for their music.

TREBLE STAFF

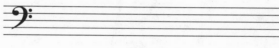

Some instruments play only notes that sound **LOW**. These instruments use the **BASS STAFF** for their music.

BASS STAFF

The **EXPLORATIONS** tape is used whenever you see the  symbol on the page. Listen to the tape for examples of sounds of different instruments that play **high** notes, **low** notes, and the full range from **high** to **low**.

1. Circle the **staff** you think would be used for the instruments you hear.

A.

B.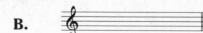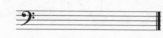

C.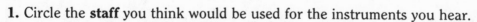

EXPLORE BONUS Which instruments did you hear on the tape? Write the correct letter names beside the pictures.

 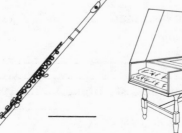 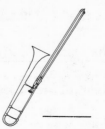 

_____   _____   _____   _____   _____

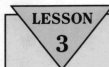

LESSON 3

LETTER NAMES ON THE STAFF

Each note written on the staff has a name that is a letter of the **MUSIC ALPHABET.** This alphabet uses only the letters **A B C D E F G**, repeating as the notes go up the staff.

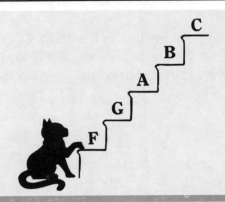

1. The **treble staff** below shows all the notes on the staff. Fill in the missing letters using the music alphabet—**A B C D E F G A B C D E F G.**

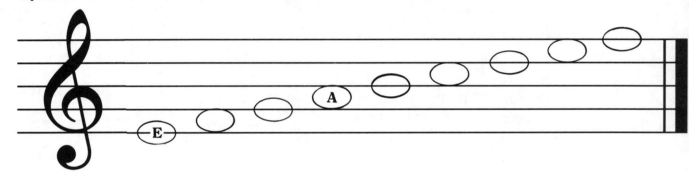

2. Color all the notes written on **lines** on the **treble staff red.**

   The names of the **treble staff lines** are ____   ____   ____   ____   ____.

3. Color all the notes written on **spaces** on the **treble staff blue.**

   The names of the **treble staff spaces** are ____   ____   ____   ____.

4. The **bass staff** below shows all the notes on the staff. Fill in the missing letters using the music alphabet—A B C D E F G A B C D E F G.

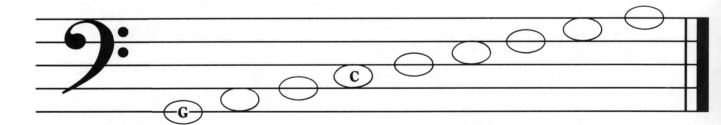

5. Color all the notes written on **lines** on the **bass staff red.**

   The names of the **bass staff lines** are ____   ____   ____   ____   ____.

6. Color all the notes written on **spaces** on the **bass staff blue.**

   The names of the **bass staff spaces** are ____   ____   ____   ____.

NOTES ON THE STAFF

Now you are ready to discover how the **lines** and **spaces**, **treble** and **bass clefs**, and **letter names** you have learned work together to write notes on the staff correctly.

1. A. Draw a **treble clef** on the empty staff below.
   B. Draw notes on each **line** on the staff, going from bottom to top.
   C. Write the correct **letter name** for each note inside the note as shown.
       (You discovered these letter names on page 8, number 2.)

E

2. A. Draw a **treble clef** on the empty staff below.
   B. Draw notes on each **space** on the staff, going from bottom to top.
   C. Write the correct **letter name** for each note inside the note as shown.
       (You discovered these letter names on page 8, number 3.)

F

3. A. Draw a **bass clef** on the empty staff below.
   B. Draw notes on each **line** on the staff, going from bottom to top.
   C. Write the correct **letter name** for each note inside the note as shown.
       (You discovered these letter names on page 8, number 5.)

G

4. A. Draw a **bass clef** on the empty staff below.
   B. Draw notes on each **space** on the staff, going from bottom to top.
   C. Write the correct **letter name** for each note inside the note as shown.
       (You discovered these letter names on page 8, number 6.)

A

PRACTICE PAGE

TREBLE STAFF LINES

TREBLE STAFF SPACES

1. Write the correct letter names below the notes written on this **treble staff**.
They should spell words.

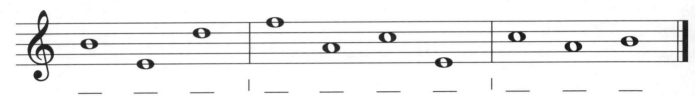

___ ___ | ___ ___ ___ | ___ ___ ___

2. Draw the notes on the **treble staff** using lines or spaces to fit the words.

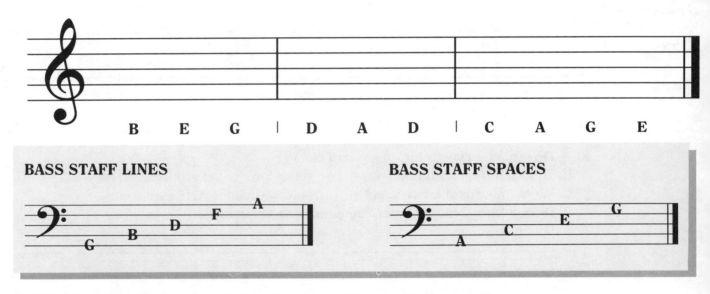

B   E   G | D   A   D | C   A   G   E

BASS STAFF LINES

BASS STAFF SPACES

3. Write the correct letter names below the notes written on this **bass staff**.
They should spell words.

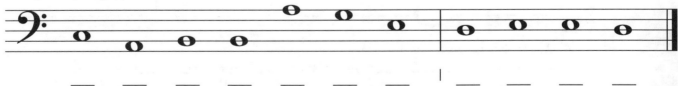

___ ___ ___ ___ ___ | ___ ___ ___ ___

4. Draw the notes on the **bass staff** using lines or spaces to fit the words below.

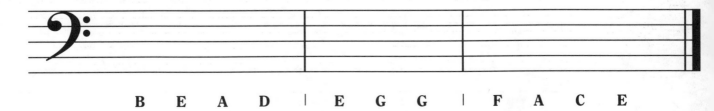

B   E   A   D | E   G   G | F   A   C   E

EXPLORE

It is fun to make up **your own** music words using the notes on the staff.

1. The music alphabet is shown below. Make up words using only these letters and write them on the lines below. The first word is given as an example.

A B C D E F G

My music words:

_____ FEED _____   _____   _____

_____   _____   _____

_____   _____   _____

2. Draw a **treble clef** on the staff below. Choose three words from your list and draw them on the treble staff using notes on the lines and spaces you have learned.

**My music
words:** _____   _____   _____

3. Draw a **bass clef** on the staff below. Choose three words from your list and draw them on the bass staff using notes on the lines and spaces you have learned.

**My music
words:** _____   _____   _____

Use the staff below for extra music words you have discovered.

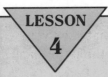

LESSON 4

MUSIC STORIES

A different way to practice the letter names on the staff is to work on a **MUSIC STORY**.

1. Fill in the letter names of the music words in the following story.

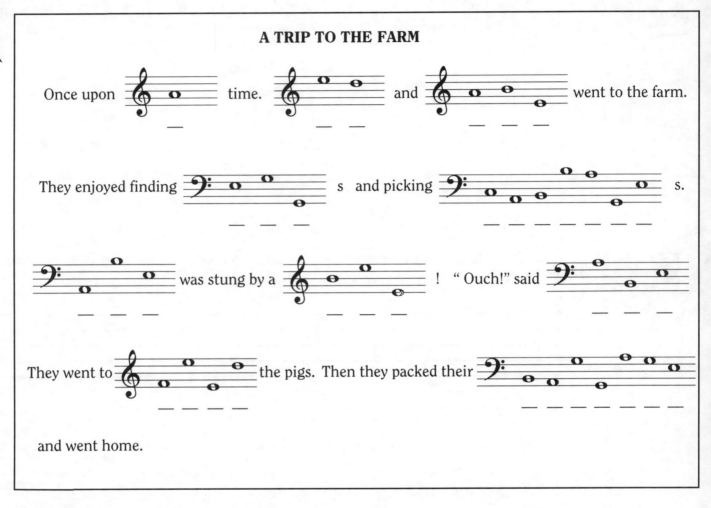

A TRIP TO THE FARM

Once upon ___ time. ___ and ___ went to the farm.

They enjoyed finding ___ s and picking ___ s.

___ was stung by a ___ ! " Ouch!" said ___

They went to ___ the pigs. Then they packed their ___

and went home.

2. Now it is your turn to create your own **music story**. First, copy below the music words you discovered on page 11.

_____

_____

3. Now use your imagination and write a story connecting as many of the words from the list above into your story. Underline the music words.

_____

_____

_____

Write your music story below, using the manuscript paper to write the notes on the staff that spell your music words. Put in blanks for letter names under each note. Let your friends try to write the letter names of **your** music story! Draw a picture above your story.

Title: _____

By: _____**Date:** _____

EXPLORE Write another music story on page 59.

LESSON 5

NOTES IN RHYTHMS

Now that you have put notes onto the staff correctly, you can learn to fit these notes to the **RHYTHM** of music. **Rhythm** is based on the natural beat of music.

QUARTER NOTE = 1 BEAT   ♩ = 1 BEAT

The rhythm below shows **QUARTER NOTES** in groups of 4 beats in **MEASURES** separated by **BAR LINES** and ending with a **DOUBLE BAR**.

1. Clap the rhythm below while listening to the **EXPLORATIONS** tape. Say "ta" with each **quarter note** as you clap.

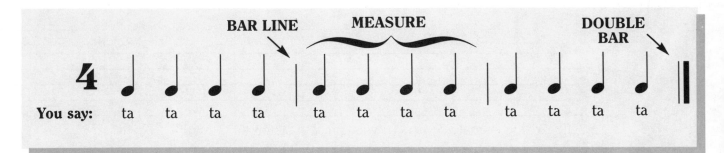

Did you end exactly with the tape? _____

2. Draw **quarter** notes on the line below as shown. Be careful to draw the **STEM** on the **right** side of the **NOTEHEAD**.

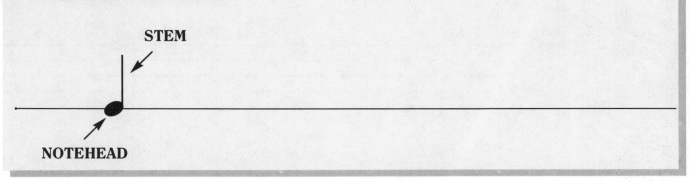

HALF NOTE = 2 BEATS    **= 2 BEATS**

A **HALF NOTE holds for 2 beats**. When clapping rhythms with a **half note,** say the word "half-note" as you clap. The sign means you hold your hands and bob them to the beat to show the second beat.

3. Clap the rhythm below while listening to the **EXPLORATIONS** tape.

You say:	half - note	half - note	ta	ta	half - note	half - note	half - note
You:	clap - bob	clap - bob	clap	clap	clap - bob	clap - bob	clap - bob

4. Draw **half notes** in the space between the lines below as shown. Watch for proper **stems.**

←— **STEM**

NOTEHEAD

5. The rhythm exercise below lets you clap and stamp to and ♩ . Try it!

CLAP

STAMP

EXPLORE Write your own rhythm using ♩ and ♩ below. Each measure should have 4 beats.

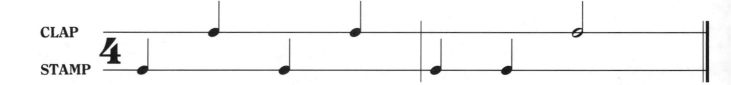

4

Now draw your rhythm on the two-line staff below, creating a rhythm exercise to enjoy.

CLAP

STAMP

WP350

A RHYTHM WORKOUT

1. Clap with the metronome and say the words or syllables **out loud.**
2. Clap with the metronome and "think" the words or syllables.
3. Keep the steady beat "inside" with no metronome and "think" the words or syllables while clapping the rhythms.
4. **Step** the steady beat while clapping and listening to the rhythms on the **EXPLORATIONS** tape—a final check to your workout!

Metronome: 1 beat = 80

A.

ta ta half-note half-note half-note ta ta ta ta ta ta half-note

B.

C.

D.

EXPLORE Share this **Rhythm Workout** with several friends.
1. One person can clap rhythm A while another steps to rhythm B.
2. One person can tap legs (patschen) to rhythm C while another snaps fingers to rhythm D.
3. A **super challenge**—all rhythms together with these rhythm sounds!

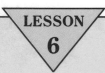

LESSON 6

MORE NOTES AND A REST

DOTTED HALF NOTE = 3 BEATS   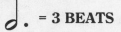 **= 3 BEATS**

The **DOTTED HALF NOTE holds for 3 beats.** When clapping rhythms with a dotted half note, you can say **"half-note-dot"** to each note, clapping and bobbing as shown.

1. Clap the rhythms below while listening to the **EXPLORATIONS** tape.

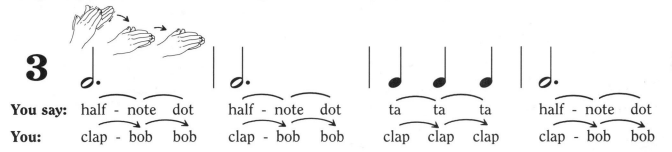

You say: half - note   dot   half - note   dot   ta   ta   ta   half - note   dot
You: clap - bob   bob   clap - bob   bob   clap clap clap   clap - bob   bob

2. Draw **dotted half notes** on the line below as shown. Draw the proper placement of the **stem** and **notehead** and don't forget the **dot**!

3. The rhythms below are in groups of 4 beats and 3 beats. Try another **Rhythm Workout** with these rhythms using the directions given on page 16. Check your workout with the **EXPLORATIONS** tape.

Metronome: 1 beat = 80

A.

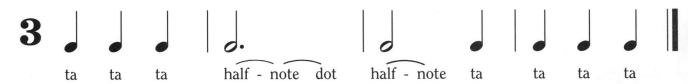

ta   ta   ta   half - note   dot   half - note   ta   ta   ta   ta

B.

C.

WHOLE NOTE = 4 BEATS **o** = 4 BEATS

The **WHOLE NOTE holds for 4 beats.** When clapping rhythms with a whole note, you can say the words **"hold-that-whole-note"** to each note, clapping and bobbing as shown below.

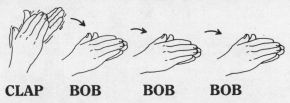

CLAP   BOB   BOB   BOB

4. Clap the rhythms below while listening to the **EXPLORATIONS** tape.

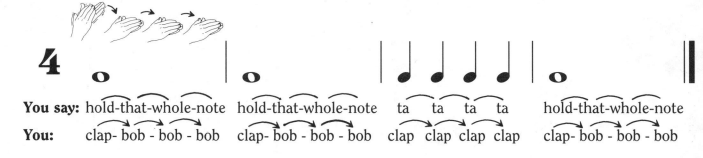

You say: hold-that-whole-note hold-that-whole-note ta ta ta ta hold-that-whole-note

You: clap- bob - bob - bob clap- bob - bob - bob clap clap clap clap clap- bob - bob - bob

5. Draw **whole notes** in the space between the lines below as shown.

QUARTER REST = 1 BEAT   **𝄾** = 1 BEAT

The **QUARTER REST shows one beat of REST.** When you see a **quarter rest** in rhythms, you can say the word "rest" in a whisper with your hands apart and NOT clapping. Rests show us silence in the music.

"REST"

6. Clap the following while listening to the **EXPLORATIONS** tape:

You say: ta ta "rest" ta ta "rest" ta ta ta "rest" ta "rest"

You: clap clap open clap clap open clap clap clap open clap open

7. Draw **quarter rests** on the full staff below as shown.

TRACE   YOUR TURN

8. Putting it together! Clap the following rhythms below that combine ♩ ♩ ♩. o 𝄽 .
Use the **Rhythm Workout** ideas you have learned. Check your workout with the **EXPLORATIONS** tape.

A.

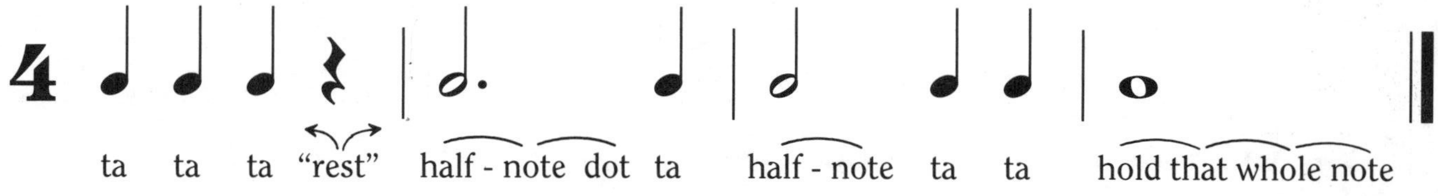

ta   ta   ta   "rest"   half - note dot   ta   half - note   ta   ta   hold that whole note

B.

C.

D.

How did you do on this rhythm challenge?

SUPER JOB ☐   DOING O.K. ☐   NEED MORE WORK ☐

EXPLORE Your turn! Write your own rhythms below using ♩ ♩ ♩. o 𝄽

Remember: **4** = 4 beats in each measure   **3** = 3 beats in each measure

A.

3

B.

4

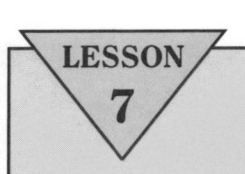

LESSON 7

TIME SIGNATURES

The **TIME SIGNATURE** shows how many beats are in each measure in the music. You have clapped to groups of 4 beats and groups of 3 beats. The proper way of showing this in music is:

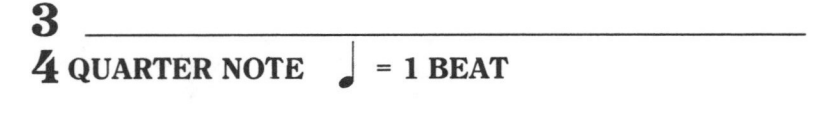

4 4 BEATS IN EACH MEASURE
4 QUARTER NOTE ♩ = 1 BEAT

The TOP number tells how many beats are in each measure.
The BOTTOM number tells what kind of note = 1 beat. (4 = ♩)

1. Fill in the line that explains the **time signature** written below, using the rule above as a clue.

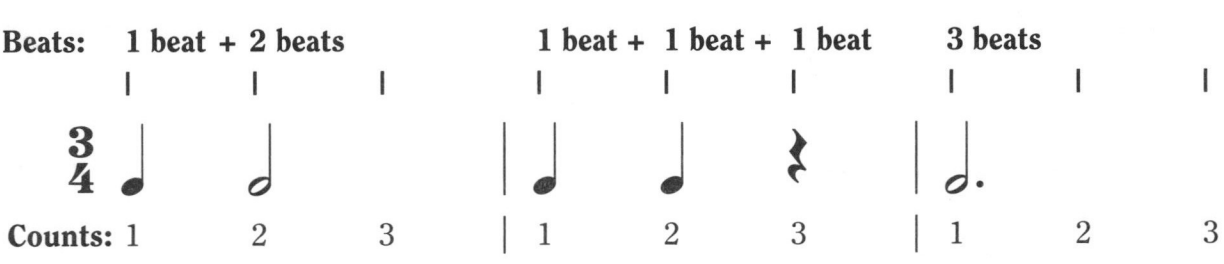

3 _____
4 QUARTER NOTE ♩ = 1 BEAT

Beats: 1 beat + 2 beats   1 beat + 1 beat + 1 beat   3 beats

Counts: 1   2   3 | 1   2   3 | 1   2   3

2. Clap the rhythms below **three ways:**

 1. "Think" the words and syllables you have learned as you clap.
 2. Count the numbers below the measures **out loud** as you clap.
 3. "Think" the numbers below the measures as you clap.

Check your work with the **EXPLORATIONS** tape

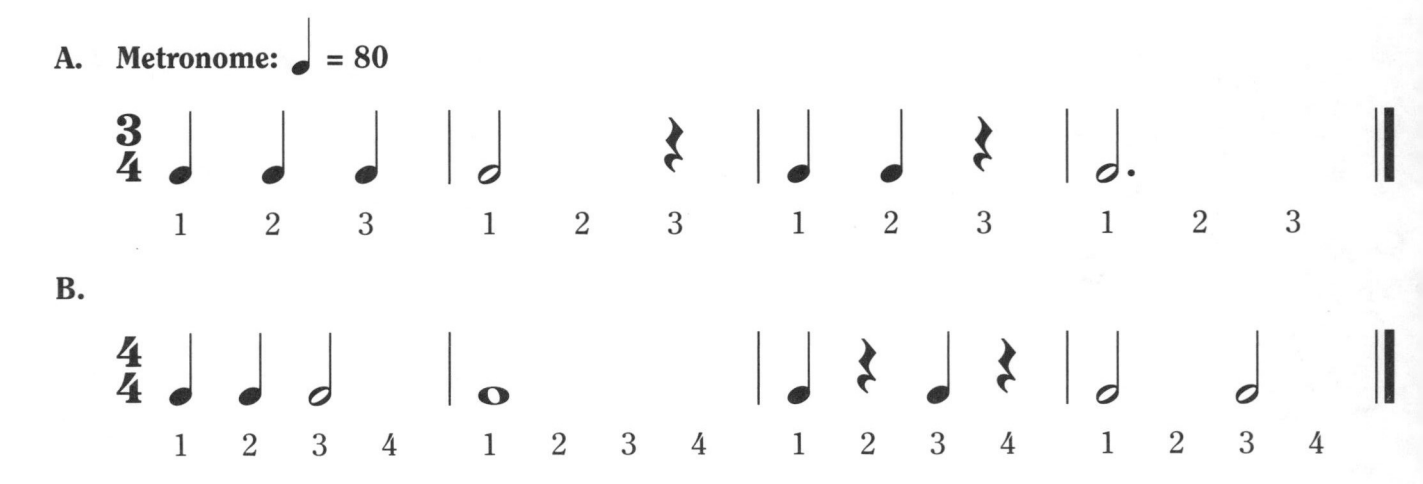

A. Metronome: ♩ = 80

3 4 1 2 3 | 1 2 3 | 1 2 3 | 1 2 3

B.

4 4 1 2 3 4 | 1 2 3 4 | 1 2 3 4 | 1 2 3 4

3. Write the counts below each measure to match the **time signatures** given.

A.

$\frac{4}{4}$ ♩ ♩ ♩ ♩ | ♩ ♩ | ♩ 𝄽 ♩ ♩ | 𝅝 ‖

Write the counts: *1   2   3   4* _____

B.

$\frac{3}{4}$ ♩ ♩ | ♩. | ♩ ♩ 𝄽 | ♩ ♩ ‖

Write the counts: _____

C.

$\frac{4}{4}$ ♩ ♩ | ♩ ♩ ♩ 𝄽 | ♩. ♩ | 𝅝 ‖

Write the counts: _____

4. Discover the correct **time signature** of the measures below:

If the counts = 3 beats, draw a $\frac{3}{4}$.   If the counts = 4 beats, draw a $\frac{4}{4}$.

To discover the correct **time signature:**
  1. Write the counts below each measure. This will let you discover how many beats are in each measure.
  2. Place the correct time signature in the boxes.

A.

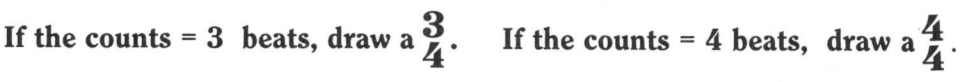

☐ ♩ ♩ ♩ | ♩ ♩ ♩ | ♩ 𝄽 ♩ | ♩. ‖

Counts: _____

B.

☐ ♩ ♩ | 𝅝 | ♩ 𝄽 ♩ | 𝅝 ‖

Counts: _____

C.

☐ ♩ ♩ | ♩ 𝄽 ♩ | ♩. | 𝄽 ♩ ‖

Counts: _____

PRACTICE PAGE

You can have fun solving a few problems on this Practice Page. Each example has a different problem that needs your help. Good Luck!

1. Help! The measures below are missing notes and we need your help to **fill each measure to match the correct number of beats with** ♩ ♩ ♩ . o . The **time signatures** will give you a musical clue.

A.

$\frac{3}{4}$

1   2   3   1   2   3   1   2   3   1   2   3

B.

$\frac{4}{4}$

1   2   3   4   1   2   3   4   1   2   3   4

C.

$\frac{3}{4}$

1   2   3   1   2   3   1   2   3   1   2   3

D.

$\frac{4}{4}$

1   2   3   4   1   2   3   4   1   2   3   4

2. Another problem! The measures below are missing the counts below each measure. **Write the correct counts**, looking at the **time signature** and notes in each measure.

A.

$\frac{3}{4}$

Write the counts: _____

B.

$\frac{4}{4}$

Write the counts: _____

3. Now the measures are missing **bar lines** and **double bars** at the end! To solve this problem you must:
   A. Look at the **time signature** to see how many beats are in each measure.
   B. Write the counts below each measure.
   C. Draw the bar lines as you discover each full measure and end with a double bar.

A.

Write the counts: _____

B.

Write the counts: _____

4. A real problem—empty measures! **Your** job is to fill them properly with notes and rests and write counts below each measure. Thank you!

A.

$\frac{3}{4}$

Write the counts: _____

B.

$\frac{4}{4}$

Write the counts: _____

EXPLORE A reward for your difficult task! The two-line rhythm staff below uses a rhythm with clapping and stamping as shown. It's fun to do—try it!

CLAP

STAMP $\frac{3}{4}$

EXPLORE BONUS Your turn to create a rhythm exercise below.

CLAP

STAMP $\frac{3}{4}$

LESSON 8

LISTEN, AND CREATE RHYTHMS

You are ready to listen to rhythms like a **MUSICAL DETECTIVE!**

1. Listen to the **EXPLORATIONS** tape for rhythms that may be the **SAME** or **DIFFERENT** from the rhythms written below. Circle the correct answer.

A.

SAME   DIFFERENT

B.

SAME   DIFFERENT

C.

SAME   DIFFERENT

D.

SAME   DIFFERENT

Rhythms have a natural **ACCENT** or stronger beat on the first beat of the measure.

2. Listen to the following examples on the **EXPLORATIONS** tape.

ACCENT

STRONG   weak   weak   weak   **STRONG**   (weak)   weak   weak

ACCENT

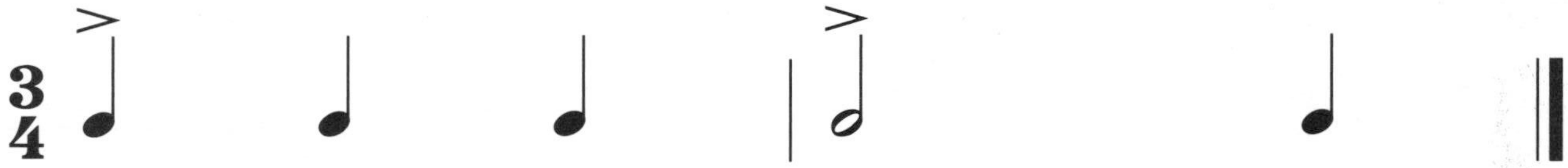

STRONG   weak   weak   **STRONG**   (weak)   weak

3. Listen to the **EXPLORATIONS** tape for examples of rhythms in $\frac{4}{4}$ and $\frac{3}{4}$
Circle what you hear.

A. $\frac{4}{4}$ $\frac{3}{4}$ C. $\frac{4}{4}$ $\frac{3}{4}$

B. $\frac{4}{4}$ $\frac{3}{4}$ D. $\frac{4}{4}$ $\frac{3}{4}$

4. Just for fun, get up and move around to some rhythm exercises. In the exercises below, do the following movements to each note or rest:

♩	𝄽	˝	♩.
STEP	**TOUCH HEAD**	**TOUCH TOES**	**STRETCH HIGH**

Metronome: Try three different ways: **SLOW** ♩ = 76 **MEDIUM** ♩ = 92 **FAST** ♩ = 108

A.

B.

C. Your turn! Write a rhythm below that would be fun to do with movements.

5. The rhythm from number **4 A** is written below on a two-line rhythm staff. Share the fun with a friend or your teacher. One person or group can do the movements to 4 A and the other can do 5 A. Add **accents** for extra interest. Take the challenge!

A.

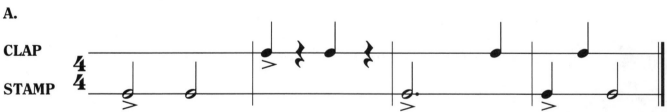

CLAP

STAMP

B. Your turn! Write the rhythm you created in number **4 C** below. Enjoy it with friends again.

CLAP

STAMP

EXPLORE Can you think of new movements to use to describe the notes and rest below?
Try the exercises above with **your** movements.

♩	𝄽	˝	♩.
_____	_____	_____	_____

EXPLORE

You can now explore the music below to find all the musical ideas you have learned.

Polka **by Dmitri Kabalevsky** (melody only)

Time to investigate! Look carefully at the musical example above to discover each answer.

1. The time signature for the piece is ⬜ . This tells us that each measure contains

_____ beats.

The _____ note = 1 beat
(See page 20 for clues.)

2. The piece is written in what staff? Circle: TREBLE   BASS   GRAND STAFF

3. The circled notes have the following letter names:

A. _____   B. _____   C. _____

4. How many half notes can you find in the music?   _____

5. The following measures have the exact same notes and rhythm:

_____ and _____   _____ and _____

6. Look at the rhythm written below. Can you find this rhythm pattern in the music?
Circle the pattern each time you see it. ♩ ♩ ♩

I found this pattern _____ times in the music.

BEYOND THE PAGE

Now you can look at your own music to discover details about notes on the staff and rhythms that you have learned in **EXPLORATIONS**.

Investigate the music you are learning in lessons for—

1. **Time signature of the piece.** It may be different from $\frac{4}{4}$ or $\frac{3}{4}$.

2. **Letter names of the first note, or notes, in the piece.**
   (Include treble and bass staff notes if you play a keyboard instrument)

3. **Repeated rhythm patterns in the piece.** Draw the pattern and write the measure numbers where you found this pattern.

MY MUSICAL INVESTIGATION

Title	Composer	Time sig.	1st note(s)	Rhythm pattern	Where?

Other musical "clues" I discovered in my investigation:

_____

_____

_____

Bravo! EXCELLENT detective work!

PRACTICE PAGE

Use these pages to practice all the ideas you have learned in **UNIT 1.** You can draw clefs, notes, and rests, or drill the letter names of notes on the staff. Also write rhythms in different time signatures. This will be excellent preparation for the following **TEST YOUR SKILLS** for **UNIT 1.**

TREBLE STAFF LINES   **TREBLE STAFF SPACES**

BASS STAFF LINES   **BASS STAFF SPACES**

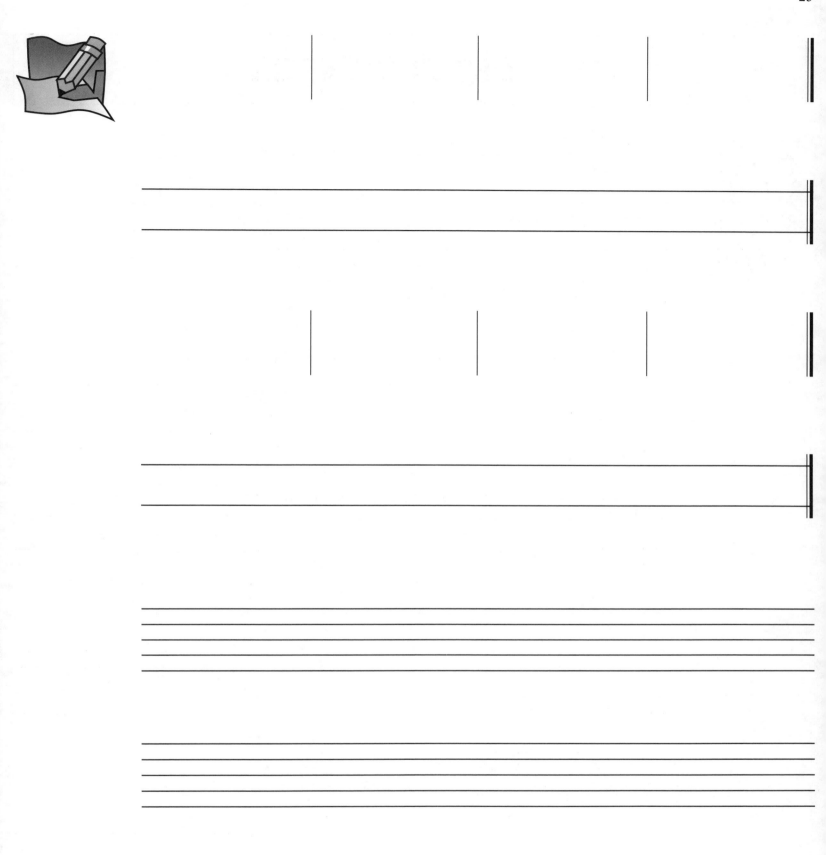

_____ *Your Score*

TEST YOUR SKILLS

1. Draw a **treble clef** on the staff below. **Draw notes on lines** around the dots shown. **Write the letter names below each of these notes.**

_____ *of 13 points*

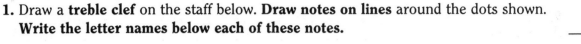

2. Write in the correct letter names below the notes written on the **treble staff** below.

_____ *of 8 points*

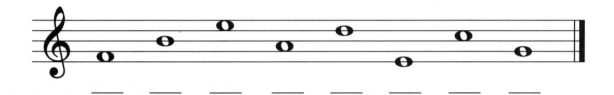

3. Draw a **bass clef** on the staff below. **Draw notes on spaces** around the dots shown. **Write the letter names below each of these notes.**

_____ *of 13 points*

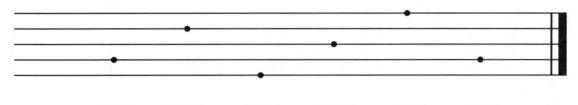

4. Write in the correct letter names below the notes written on the **bass staff** below.

_____ *of 8 points*

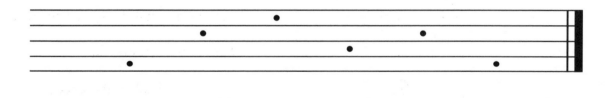

5. Draw the notes to fit the words below.

_____ *of 8 points*

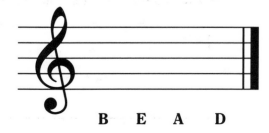

B   E   A   D

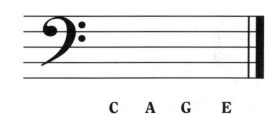

C   A   G   E

6. Complete each measure with **ONE note or rest. Write in the counts** below each measure.

_____ *of 20 points*

A.

3/4 ♩ ♩ | ♩ 𝅗𝅥 | 𝄽 | | ♩ ‖

Write
the counts:_____

B.

4/4 𝅗𝅥 | ♩ 𝄽 ♩ | 𝅗𝅥. | ♩ | ‖

Write
the counts:_____

7. Draw a line from the symbol or note to the words that describe it below.
Circle the symbol or note that is not connected to words.

_____ *of 8 points*

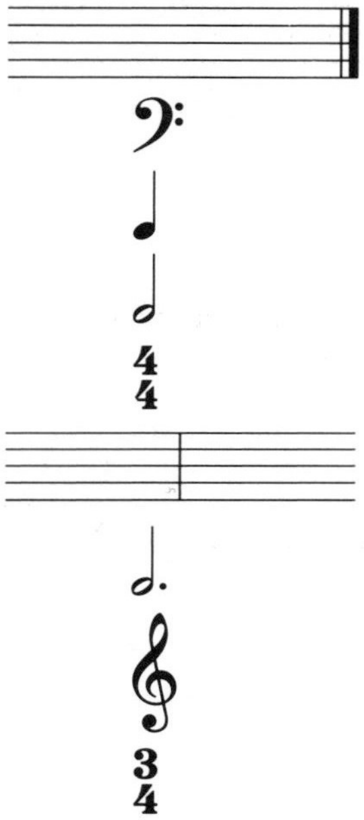

𝄄

𝄢

♩

𝅗𝅥

4/4

�:

𝅗𝅥.

𝄞

3/4

holds for 2 beats

used on the staff that has high notes

3 beats to each measure

holds for 3 beats

used on the staff that has low notes

4 beats to each measure

shows "the end" of the music

8. Draw bar lines and a double bar in the correct places in these examples. Look carefully at the time
signatures and **write in the counts** below each measure.

_____ *of 14 points*

3/4 ♩ ♩ ♩ 𝅗𝅥 𝄽 𝅗𝅥. ♩ ♩   **4/4** 𝅗𝅥 ♩ 𝄽 ♩ ♩ 𝅗𝅥 𝅗𝅥. 𝄽

Write
the counts:_____   _____

9. Fill in the measures below with  ♩ 𝅗𝅥 𝅗𝅥. 𝅝 𝄽 . **Write in the counts** below each measure.

_____ *of 8 points*

4/4 | | | ‖

Write
the counts: _____

UNIT 2
LESSON 9

MELODY SHAPES

Music is made up of notes that move up and down the staff. This movement makes a shape that is called a **MELODY**. Melodies move by **STEPS** and **SKIPS**.

The **EXPLORATIONS** tape will play the **MELODY SHAPES** below. As you listen, trace the melody with your pencil point. All melodies will be moving by **steps**.

Melody moving UP by STEPS.

Melody moving DOWN by STEPS.

Melody moving UP and DOWN by STEPS.

Melody using REPEATED notes.

1. Melody shapes: Listen and trace these melodies that combine the shapes from above.

A.

B.

C.

2. Your turn! Draw a melody shape on the staff below using only steps. The starting note is written. Play this melody on your instrument.

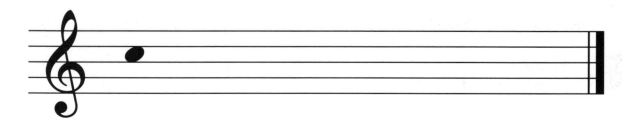

The melody shapes below move by **skips**. Listen to the **EXPLORATIONS** tape as you trace them with your pencil point.

Melody moving UP by SKIPS.

Melody moving DOWN by SKIPS.

Melody moving UP and DOWN by SKIPS.

3. Melody shapes: Listen and trace these melodies that combine the shapes from above.

A.

B.

4. Your turn! Draw a melody shape on the staff below using only **skips**. The starting note is written. Play this melody on your instrument.

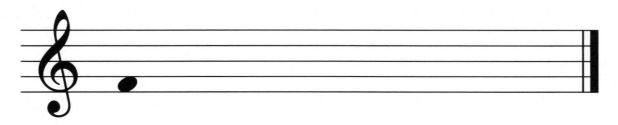

5. Write the letter names below the following **melody shapes**.

A. Melody moving UP by STEP.

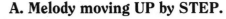

B. Melody moving UP by SKIP.

6. Circle the letters of the music alphabet that match the letters in number 5 A and B.

A. Steps

G   A   B   C   D   E

B. Skips

G   A   B   C   D   E

LESSON 10
LISTEN, AND CREATE MELODIES

It is time to be a Musical Detective for melody shapes!

The **EXPLORATIONS** tape will play three of the **melody shapes** written below.
Before starting the tape, please read these directions!

1. Before listening to the tape, trace the melody shapes with your pencil, singing the shape out loud or "in your head," listening for steps and skips.

2. **Do not trace the melody** when you listen to the tape the first time. Try to hear the melody from the tape "in your head" as you hear it played.

3. Sing the melody you heard out loud or "in your head" and match it to a written melody.

4. Write the correct letter names on the lines.

1. Do you hear A or B? _____

A.

B.

2. Do you hear C or D? _____

C.

D.

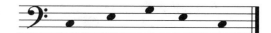

3. Do you hear E or F? _____

E.

F.

4. You will hear three notes moving by **step** or by **skip**. Circle what you hear.

A.	STEP	SKIP	**B.**	STEP	SKIP
C.	STEP	SKIP	**D.**	STEP	SKIP

5. Now it is time for you to be a **COMPOSER**! This page has room for two melody shapes—one using only **steps** and one using only **skips**.

HOW TO COMPOSE MELODY SHAPES
   A. Draw the clef that matches your instrument on the empty staff below.
   B. Find a note that is comfortable to play as your melody's starting note. Write it on the staff with only a notehead - ● .
   C. Experiment moving up and down only by **step** on your instrument until you find a melody that sounds interesting. You can repeat notes if you like.
   D. **Repeat** this melody over and over until you know it well. Keep it short and simple.
   E. Write the notes on the staff.

My **Stepping** Melody Title: _____

6. Follow the same directions to compose a melody shape using only **skips**.

My **Skipping** Melody Title: _____

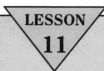

TRIADS ON C, G, AND F

TRIADS are formed from 3 notes that are written **skips** apart. You can draw **Major triads** written on C, F, and G from what you have learned. You will learn to write other triads in **EXPLORATIONS IN MUSIC, Book 2.**

To draw **TRIADS** on the staff, think of a **snowman!**

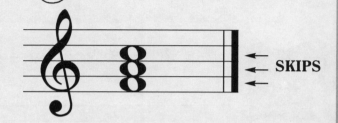

SKIPS →

SKIPS ←

Triad built on LINES

Triad built on SPACES

The triads written below will use a **new note on the staff.**

Notice the note written on its own line: This is **MIDDLE C.**

EXPLORE Why is this note called middle C? Investigate the keyboard pictured on page 6 for clues. Explain your answer to your teacher.

C MAJOR TRIAD

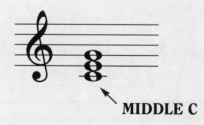

MIDDLE C

1. Write the **C Major triad** below. Be careful that your "snowman" stands straight!

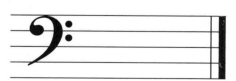

EXPLORE The letter names of these notes are _____ _____ and _____ .

F MAJOR TRIAD

2. Draw the **F Major triad** below.

EXPLORE The letter name of the notes are _____ _____ and _____ .

G MAJOR TRIAD

3. Draw the **G MAJOR TRIAD** below.

 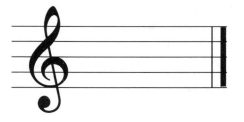

EXPLORE The letter names of these notes are _____ _____ and _____ .

4. Circle the letter names of the notes in the music alphabet that match the notes in the triads below.

C MAJOR TRIAD	C	D	E	F	G	A	B
F MAJOR TRIAD	F	G	A	B	C	D	E
G MAJOR TRIAD	G	A	B	C	D	E	F

PRACTICE PAGE

1. Write a **melody shape** moving up and down by **step**.

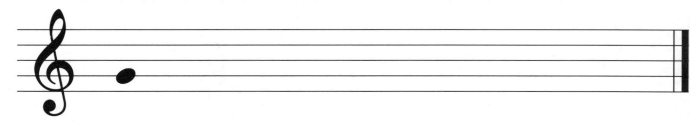

2. Draw the following **triads**.

C MAJOR   F MAJOR   G MAJOR

3. Draw a **melody shape** moving up and down by **skip**.

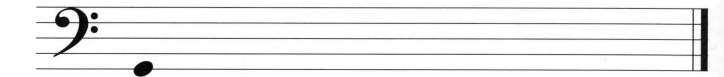

4. Draw a **melody shape** moving by **step** or **skip** using only these notes.

EXPLORE Play the different **triads** you have learned on your instrument. Find the triad that would sound best as an **ACCOMPANIMENT** (harmonies that are background notes) to the melody in number 4. Write it below in the treble staff.

 Use the space below for extra drill writing **triads** and **melody shapes** to prepare for **TEST YOUR SKILLS** for **UNIT 2**

EXPLORE

The music below shows the melody shape of a piece titled **Etude** by Dmitri Kabalevsky. The rhythm of the notes is not shown.

1. Trace the melody shape **with your fingertip** as you listen to the **EXPLORATIONS** tape perform this melody shape. **Be careful**—it goes quite fast!

Melody Shape of Etude by Dmitri Kabalevsky (opening measures)

WOW! Why not rewind and try it again!

Now answer the questions below investigating what you heard and what you see.

2. The melody shape of **Etude** moved mostly by (circle) STEPS   SKIPS

3. The highest note the melody plays has the letter name _____. It plays _____ times.

4. There are three **very big skips** in the melody shape. Circle them in the music.

5. Find the new symbol in the music and draw it in the box.
   Investigate this symbol with your teacher.

6. Draw a box around the **repeated notes** in the music.
   They have the letter name _____.

LISTENING FOR MUSICAL COLOR

Now you can listen to the *Etude* performed with both the **MELODY** and **ACCOMPANIMENT** (background notes) and with **DYNAMICS**.

DYNAMICS color the music by making it **loud** or **soft** and gradually getting louder and softer.

$\boldsymbol{p}$ $\boldsymbol{f}$

soft   loud   gradually getting louder   gradually getting softer

piano   forte   crescendo   decrescendo

BONUS *Piano* and *forte* mean soft and loud in what language? Investigate!

7. Follow the "color path" below **with your eyes** as you listen for **dynamics.**

DYNAMIC COLOR PATH for *Etude* :

$$\boldsymbol{p} <\!> \boldsymbol{p} <\!> \boldsymbol{p} <\!> \boldsymbol{p} <\!> \boldsymbol{p} <\!\boldsymbol{f}$$

8. Now it is time to **move around** to this melody! As the music begins $\boldsymbol{p}$, squat down low making a ball of yourself. As the music  slowly stand up and raise your arms. Reach high overhead when the music reaches $\boldsymbol{f}$. Enjoy this "ear and body" exercise!

Get the tape ready and get into the position for $\boldsymbol{p}$. Begin!

EXPLORE BONUS The **EXPLORATIONS** tape will play another melody and accompaniment for you to discover dynamic color at a slower tempo. Listen and draw your own **dynamic color path** below. Then move around again for another musical "ear and body" exercise!

My dynamic color path:

TEST YOUR SKILLS

1. Circle words for the correct answer about each **melody shape.**

_____ *of 6 points*

A.

The melody is moving UP   DOWN   UP & DOWN   by SKIPS   STEPS

B.

The melody is moving UP   DOWN   UP & DOWN   by SKIPS   STEPS

C.

The melody is moving UP   DOWN   UP & DOWN   by SKIPS   STEPS

2. Draw **melody shapes** from the written notes as indicated.

_____ *of 20 points*

Moving UP by STEP   Moving DOWN by SKIP

EXPLORE BONUS

_____ *+ 5 points*

Letter names _____

Moving Up and Down by STEP   Moving Up and Down by SKIP

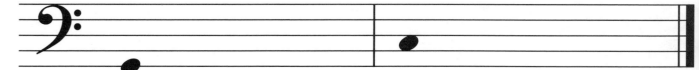

EXPLORE BONUS

_____ *+ 5 points*

Letter names _____

3. Draw the following **triads**:

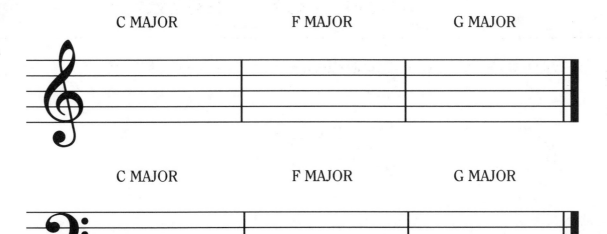

C MAJOR   F MAJOR   G MAJOR

C MAJOR   F MAJOR   G MAJOR

4. Putting it together!

    A. Write a melody shape on the **treble staff** using **steps AND skips** in your melody. Use only the notes written. You can move up and down and repeat notes if you like.   ____ *of 6 points*

USE THESE NOTES IN YOUR MELODY SHAPE

    B. Draw a **G Major triad** in the **bass staff**. If your instrument is a keyboard instrument, you can play both the melody shape and triad.

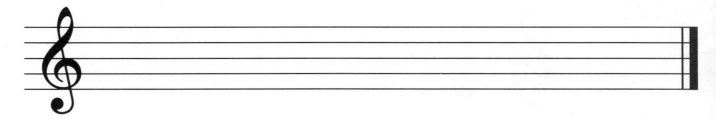

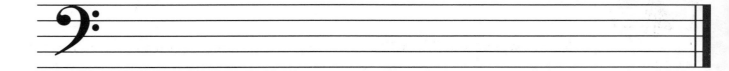

LOOK AND LISTEN

You listened for sounds that are **LOW** and **HIGH** when learning about the **treble staff** and the **bass staff.**

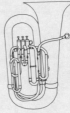 **LOW SOUNDS**  **HIGH SOUNDS**

You listened for sounds that are **LOUD** and **SOFT** when learning about dynamics.

LOUD SOUNDS 𝒇

SOFT SOUNDS 𝒑

1. Listen to the **EXPLORATIONS** tape for music that is **high or low** and **loud or soft**. Circle the clef and dynamic signs that describe what you hear.

	HIGH	LOW		LOUD	SOFT
A. The music I heard was	𝄞	𝄢	and was	𝒇	𝒑
B. The music I heard was	𝄞	𝄢	and was	𝒇	𝒑
C. The music I heard was	𝄞	𝄢	and was	𝒇	𝒑

2. Draw something in the box below that would describe a sound that is **low and soft.**
Your picture does not have to be about music.

3. Draw something in the box below to describe a sound that is **high and loud.**
Your picture does not have to be about music.

4. Listen to the **EXPLORATIONS** tape for notes that are moving **up, down,** or **up and down**.
Circle what you hear.

A.	UP	DOWN	UP & DOWN
B.	UP	DOWN	UP & DOWN
C.	UP	DOWN	UP & DOWN
D.	UP	DOWN	UP & DOWN

5. Draw something in the boxes below that shows:

STEPPING UP   STEPPING DOWN   SKIPPING UP & DOWN

EXPLORE Try this **listening challenge!** The **EXPLORATIONS** tape will play notes that are moving
by **step** or **skip**. They will be moving **up, down,** or **up and down.**

Listen carefully and circle what you hear. Good luck!

A.	STEP	SKIP	moving	UP	DOWN	UP & DOWN
B.	STEP	SKIP	moving	UP	DOWN	UP & DOWN
C.	STEP	SKIP	moving	UP	DOWN	UP & DOWN

WP350

EXPLORE

You have learned to listen carefully to melody shapes written on the staff. Now have some fun listening to the shape of melodies by drawing them simply as a line—free and easy!

The **EXPLORATIONS** tape will play several melodies that will be fun to "draw" as you listen to them. The picture below shows a line that might describe the melody on the tape. Listen and see how it shows the movement of what you hear.

MELODY from *Invention in F Major* by J.S. Bach

Now it is your turn! Remember there is no "correct" answer. Just listen and draw!

MELODY 1

MELODY 2

BEYOND THE PAGE

You can now investigate the music you are learning for all the things you have learned in **EXPLORATIONS IN MUSIC, Book 1.** Choose a piece you enjoy and discover the following:

Title: _____

Composer: _____ **Date:** _____

1. Copy the first measure of your piece below. Be sure to include the correct **clefs** and **time signature** that are written on each staff.

2. The **time signature** of the piece is: ☐ This means there are _____ beats in each measure and that the

   _____ note = 1 beat.

3. Write the letter name under **each note** in the measure above.

4. The **highest** note in the measure has the letter name _____.

5. The **lowest** note in the measure has the letter name _____.

6. Can you find a **step** in the measure? YES NO   Circle one step in the music and label as **step**.

7. Can you find a **skip** in the measure? YES NO   Circle one skip in the music and label as **skip**.

8. If the measure has a **melody**, describe how it moves.

    UP   DOWN   UP AND DOWN   REPEATED NOTES

9. Look through the entire piece for marks that show **dynamics**. Write what you find below.

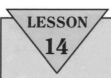

LESSON 14

MUSIC DICTIONARY

Watch the **MUSIC DICTIONARY** grow as you progress in the **EXPLORATIONS IN MUSIC**, Books 1-7.

Word	Symbol	Definition	First Found on Page (You fill in.)
ACCENT	>	A louder or stronger note or beat	24
ACCOMPANIMENT		A musical background added to a melody.	
BAR LINE		Lines separating measures of music.	
BASS CLEF	𝄢	A symbol drawn around the line F on the staff that shows notes low in pitch.	
BASS STAFF		The staff that shows notes from Middle C and lower.	
CRESCENDO		To gradually get louder	
DECRESCENDO		To gradually get softer	
DOTTED HALF NOTE	𝅗𝅥.	The note that = 3 beats in $\frac{3}{4}$ and $\frac{4}{4}$	
DOUBLE BAR		Used at the end of music. It is sometimes called "ending bar."	
FORTE	f	Loud	
GRAND STAFF		The treble staff and bass staff drawn together.	
HALF NOTE	𝅗𝅥	The note that = 2 beats in $\frac{3}{4}$ and $\frac{4}{4}$	
MEASURE		A section of the staff separated by bar lines and containing notes in groups of beats depending on the time signature.	
MELODY		A line of musical notes moving up or down that can be sung or played.	
PIANO	p	Soft	
QUARTER NOTE	𝅘𝅥	The note that = 1 beat in $\frac{3}{4}$ and $\frac{4}{4}$	
QUARTER REST	𝄽	The rest that = 1 beat in $\frac{3}{4}$ and $\frac{4}{4}$	

SKIP		Moving from one note skipping over the next on the staff–from line to line or space to space.
STAFF		A group of 5 lines and 4 spaces on which music is written.
STEP		Moving from one note to the very next on the staff - from line to space or space to line.
TIME SIGNATURE	$\frac{3}{4}$ $\frac{4}{4}$	Shows how many beats are in each measure (top number) and what type of note = 1 beat (bottom number)
TREBLE CLEF	𝄞	A symbol drawn around the line G on the staff that shows notes high in pitch.
TREBLE STAFF		The staff that shows notes from Middle C and higher.
TRIAD		Three notes that are written as skips apart.
WHOLE NOTE	𝅝	The note that = 4 beats in $\frac{3}{4}$ and $\frac{4}{4}$

USING MUSIC SYMBOLS

Draw a line from the symbol to its correct definition below:

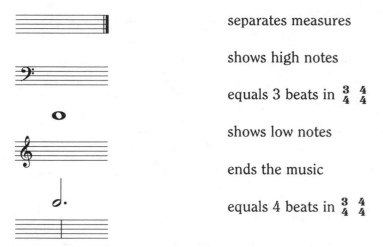

separates measures

shows high notes

equals 3 beats in $\frac{3}{4}$ $\frac{4}{4}$

shows low notes

ends the music

equals 4 beats in $\frac{3}{4}$ $\frac{4}{4}$

PRACTICE PAGE

Use this page to review both **UNITS 1, 2,** and **3** in preparation for the **FINAL TEST** on the following page.

_____ _Your Score_

TEST YOUR SKILLS

1. Write the **letter names** of the notes below.

_____ _of 8 points_

_____ _____ _____ _____ _____ _____ _____ _____

_____ _____ _____ _____ _____ _____ _____ _____

2. Add **bar lines** and a **double bar** to the following examples. **Write in the counts** below each measure.

_____ _of 8 points_

Counts: _____

3. Fill in each measure with **one note** that will complete the measure. Look carefully at the **time signature** and **write in the counts** below each measure.

_____ _of 8 points_

Counts: _____

4. Write the **counts** below each measure. Then place the correct **time signature** in the box.

_____ _of 9 points_

Counts: _____

5. Match the terms to the correct symbol. Circle the words and symbols that **do not** have partners.

_____ *of 5 points*

A. half note   _____   𝄞

B. quarter rest   _____   ◁

C. forte   _____   **3**
                           4

D. whole note   _____   𝄢

E. piano   _____   *p*

F. treble clef   _____   ♩

G. time signature   _____   𝄽

H. crescendo   _____   *f*

I. bass clef   _____   ▷

J. decrescendo   _____   𝅝

6. Draw a **treble clef** on the staff below. Draw the notes that match the letter names given.

_____ *of 7 points*

      A   E   B   F   G   C

7. Draw a **bass clef** on the staff below. Draw the notes that match the letter names given.

_____ *of 7 points*

      C   B   E   G   A   D

8. Draw a **melody shape** on the staff below that moves up by step.

_____ *of 5 points*

9. Draw a **melody shape** on the staff below that moves **up and down by skip**.

_____ *of 5 points*

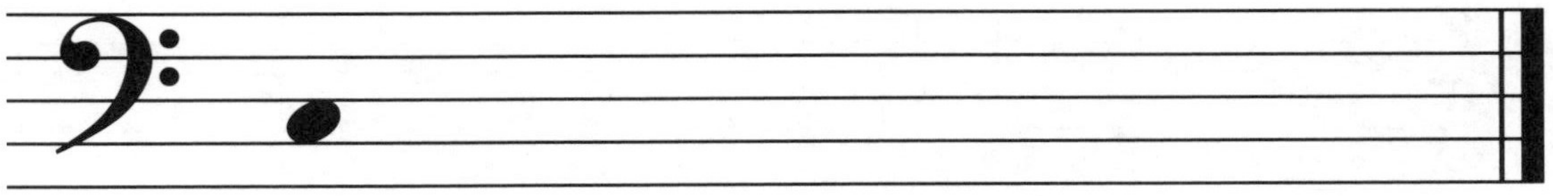

10. Draw the following **triads.**

_____ *of 6 points*

C MAJOR   F MAJOR   G MAJOR

C MAJOR   F MAJOR   G MAJOR

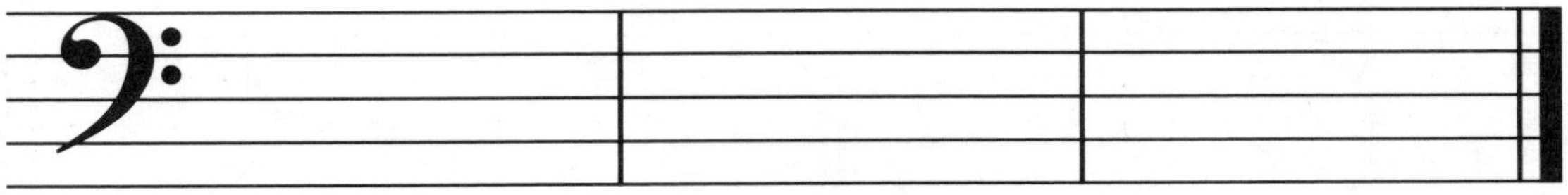

11. Fill in the measures below with the notes you have learned. Be careful to look at the **time signature.**
Write in the counts below each measure.

_____ *of 8 points*

3/4   **4/4**

Counts: _____   _____

EXPLORE BONUS Write one of your rhythms from number 11 on the two-line rhythm staff.

_____ *+ 2 points*

CLAP _____

STAMP _____

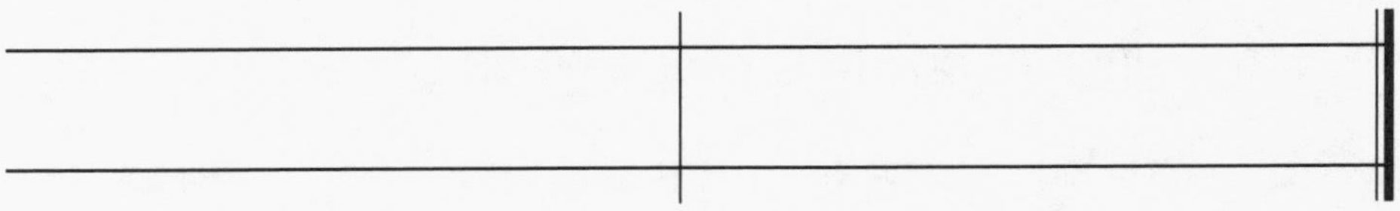

WP350

12. Find the following in the example below. Put the correct letter name in the boxes.
Note: Some boxes will be empty when you are finished.

_____ *of 6 points*

     A. dotted half note   **D.** double bar
     B. bar line   **E.** quarter note
     C. time signature   **F.** treble clef

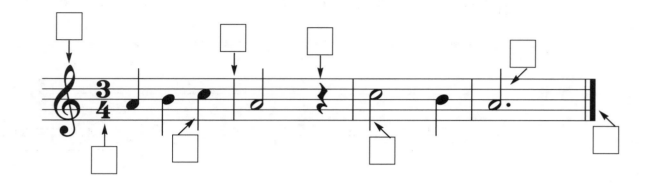

13. Listen carefully to the **EXPLORATIONS** tape!

    A. Are the notes you hear **high** or **low**? Circle what you hear.

_____ *of 4 points*

      1. HIGH   LOW   **3.**   HIGH   LOW

      2. HIGH   LOW   **4.**   HIGH   LOW

    B. Listen to the following rhythms. Is each one the **same** or **different** from the one written below?
       Circle what you hear.

_____ *of 3 points*

                                           SAME   DIFFERENT

                                           SAME   DIFFERENT

                                           SAME   DIFFERENT

    C. Listen to the following melodies that are moving **up, down,** or **up and down.** Circle what you hear.

_____ *of 4 point*

      1.   UP   DOWN   UP & DOWN

      2.   UP   DOWN   UP & DOWN

      3.   UP   DOWN   UP & DOWN

      4.   UP   DOWN   UP & DOWN

D. Identify the melodies you hear by filling in the letter names on the blanks.

1. Do you hear A or B? _____   ____ *of 3 points*

A.

B.

2. Do you hear C or D? _____

C.

D.

3. Do you hear E or F? _____

E.

F.

E. You will hear three notes moving by **step** or **skip**. Circle what you hear.   ____ *of 4 points*

    1.   STEP   SKIP   **3.**   STEP   SKIP

    2.   STEP   SKIP   **4.**   STEP   SKIP

EXPLORE BONUS You can take a **listening challenge** and **write what you hear** for rhythm and melody.

1. Rhythm: Listen to the rhythm on the tape and try to **write** what you hear. The time signature and first note are given. Only ♩ and ♩ will be used. It will be played two times.

    ____ *of + 4 points*

2. Melody: Listen to the **melody shape** played on the tape and try to **write** it below. The starting note is written. Use only noteheads ● . It will be played two times.

    ____ *of + 4 points*

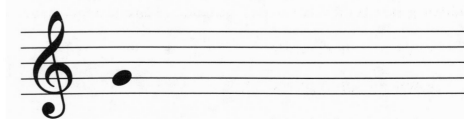

CONGRATULATIONS for learning so much! Turn the page if you want to **listen** and **explore** more!

EXTEND YOUR LISTENING

If you enjoyed the **EXPLORE BONUS** examples in **TEST YOUR SKILLS**, you may like to try a few more listening examples **writing what you hear**. ♩ ♩ ♩. and 𝅝 are used.

1. Listen to the following rhythm examples on the **EXPLORATIONS** tape and **write what you hear**. The first note is written. Each rhythm will be played two times. ♩ ♩ ♩. and 𝅝 are used.

1.

2.

3.

2. Listen to the following **melody shapes** on the **EXPLORATIONS** tape and **write what you hear.** The first notes are written. Use only noteheads ● . Each melody shape will be played two times.

1.
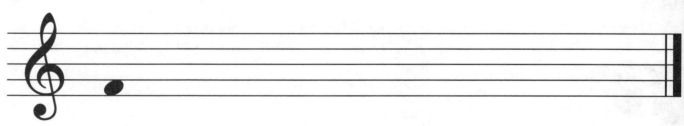

2.
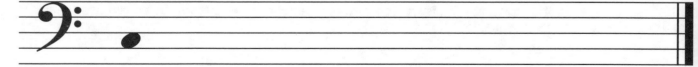

3.
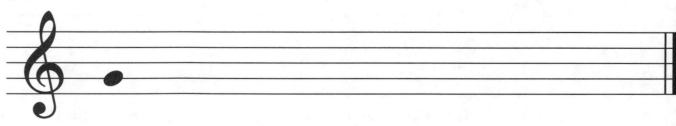

EXPLORE AND EXCEL

Write your music story below, using the manuscript paper to write the notes on the staff that spell your music words. Put in blanks for letter names under each note. Let your friends try to write the letter names of **your** music story! Draw a picture above your story.

Title: _____

By: _____ **Date:** _____

ANSWERS FOR LISTENING EXAMPLES

page 7
L1
1. A. Treble Staff
   B. Grand Staff
   C. Bass Staff

EXPLORE BONUS
   A. Violin
   B. Harpsichord
   C. Trombone

page 24
L11
1. A. SAME
   B. DIFFERENT
   C. DIFFERENT
   D. SAME

3. A. $\frac{4}{4}$
   B. $\frac{3}{4}$
   C. $\frac{4}{4}$
   D. $\frac{3}{4}$

page 34
L14
1. A
2. D
3. E
4. A. STEP
   B. SKIP
   C. SKIP
   D. STEP

page 44
L18
1. A. LOW and SOFT
   B. HIGH and SOFT
   C. HIGH and LOUD

page 45
L19
A. UP
B. UP & DOWN
C. DOWN
D. UP & DOWN

page 45
L20
A. STEP moving UP
B. SKIP moving UP & DOWN
C. STEP moving DOWN

pages 54 & 55
L22
A. 1. HIGH
   2. LOW
   3. LOW
   4. HIGH

B. 1. SAME
   2. SAME
   3. DIFFERENT

C. 1. DOWN
   2. UP & DOWN
   3. UP
   4. DOWN

D. 1. B
   2. C
   3. E

E. 1. STEP
   2. STEP
   3. SKIP
   4. SKIP

L23
EXPLORE BONUS
1. Rhythm:

2. Melody:

page 56
L24
Rhythms:

1.

2.

3.

Melodies:

1.

2.

3.

CONTENTS

At the top of each **Teacher's Guide** page you will see the correlated **Student Book** pages indicated. The Student pages are shown with the **answers** written in. You will find **OBJECTIVES** and **TEACHING TIPS**, plus **EXCEL** and **EXTEND** ideas on every page.

FEATURES OF EXPLORATIONS IN MUSIC, Books 1-7

Students explore and discover new concepts.

Each concept is used in a variety of ways, always including opportunities for creativity.

Creative experimentation encourages students to compose.

Listening examples are interwoven throughout the book and presented on the cassette. They develop aural discrimination, score analysis, and interpretation.

Cassettes allow listening to be done outside of lesson time—at home or in theory classes.

Explore sections allow students to analyze the musical score with "eye and ear" and work creatively with musical ideas.

Explore Bonus sections offer the curious student a challenge, providing motivation to work beyond what is already presented.

Beyond the Page sections offer opportunities to link the student's current repertoire directly to the concepts developed in EXPLORATIONS IN MUSIC.

Each book has **3 Units and 3 Tests**. The third test covers the entire book.

This series is developed from **Music Teachers National Association** and affiliated state organizations' theory guidelines.

Creative explorations extend the ideas of Carl Orff and Zoltan Kodály.

A **Facts to Know** page assesses the student's readiness for that book (beginning with Book 2).

The Starting Point: A Review is a miniature refresher of skills the student has learned. This clarifies student strengths and weaknesses at the start of each book.

Each book has a **similar sequence** to facilitate use in classes with students at different levels.

WHAT WILL STUDENTS DO IN *EXPLORATIONS IN MUSIC?*

WRITE
Apply each new idea they learn through writing.

INVESTIGATE
Search for new ideas in this book and in the music they perform to discover specific information.

LISTEN
Listen to the cassette to recognize new information in performed music and to develop skills through ear-training exercises. Each listening example is numbered in the book and annou   e. A bell sour of each exa

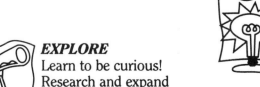
ANALYZE
Discover details in the music by analyzing with their eyes and ears.

CREATE
Experiment with their ideas by composing. Use their imagination to stretch their mind and their senses.

EXPLORE
Learn to be curious! Research and expand on musical ideas.

EXPLORATIONS IN MUSIC, TEACHER'S GUIDE 1

The **EXPLORATIONS IN MUSIC TEACHER'S GUIDES** compliment the overall approach of teaching music theory in a comprehensive way. The Guides contain creative teaching ideas for each lesson plus suggestions for exploring beyond what is on the page. Each student page is reproduced alongside the teaching ideas and, when appropriate, include answers written directly on the student pages.

The goal of **EXPLORATIONS IN MUSIC, Books 1-7** is to expand the idea of music theory to points beyond the written page, to have your students realize that the music they are performing, listening to, and composing evolves from the realm of music theory.

I believe students can best understand how music is constructed by working with each musical idea in a number of different ways—writing, listening, analyzing scores, investigating their own repertoire, experimenting with composing, and various other creative activities. With this broad understanding, your students will make connections between the study of music theory and the music they hear, perform, and create.

Joanne Haroutounian

BENEFITS FOR TEACHERS & STUDENTS

Teaching Objectives of each lesson are adjacent to the reproduced student page.

Teaching Tips with helpful strategies and activities are adjacent to the reproduced student page.

Listening examples range from solo instruments to chamber music and orchestral excerpts. A variety of instruments is used to add interest and awareness of timbre. Titles of excerpts on the cassette are included for possible follow-up listening lessons.

Extend activities extend knowledge through extra practice. These activities are helpful for students who may not grasp the concepts easily, or who need the security of extra drill.

Excel activities for each lesson offer curious students opportunities to reach a bit beyond what has been taught. These activities are helpful for the students who grasp concepts rapidly and seek challenges.

Creative student worksheets are included to augment assignments with extra fun. Permission is given to reproduce them.

C clef suggestions are included for students who play instruments in that clef.

To provide a review of **Facts to Know**, each book after the first level begins with **A Starting Point: A Review.**

A **Student Progress Chart** for recording student scores of EXPLORATIONS IN MUSIC Unit and Final Tests and your comments is on the inside front cover. Permission is given to reproduce it for your convenience and success.

A **Scope & Sequence Chart** for the entire seven-book EXPLORATIONS IN MUSIC series is on the inside back cover. It is also included in the Student Books.

JOANNE HAROUTOUNIAN

Joanne Haroutounian is a teacher and performer in Arlington, Virginia. She loves to see students grow with newfound knowledge. Her wealth of experiences in teaching, performing, and studying psychology and Orff and Kodály concepts is shared through EXPLORATIONS IN MUSIC. This theory series nurtures the concept that learning happens best when students are involved in the discovery process and can immediately apply new information.

ISBN 0-8497-9539-7

©1993 Neil A. Kjos Music Company, 4380 Jutland Drive, San Diego, California 92117.
International copyright secured. All rights reserved. Printed in U.S.A.

4

THE STAFF: LINES AND SPACES

Music is written on a music **STAFF**. The staff is made up of **LINES** and **SPACES**.

1. Count the number of **lines** you see on the staff above. There are __5__ lines.

The notes below are written on the **lines** of the staff. A line goes through the **middle** of each note. ⊸

2. Draw notes on the single line below. Remember, **the line goes through the middle of each note.**

3. Now draw notes on all the **lines** of the staff below by making a circle around the dots given. The first two notes are drawn as examples.

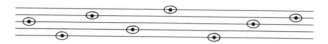

4. Notes written correctly on the **lines** of the staff **have the line going exactly through the middle of the note.** Draw an **X** on all the line notes that are drawn **incorrectly** on the staff below.

WP350

5

SPACES

5. Count the number of **spaces** between the lines you find on the staff. There are __4__ spaces.

The notes below are drawn on the **spaces** of the staff. They are placed between the lines carefully filling each space but **not crossing the lines.**

6. Draw notes in the space between the two lines below. **Remember not to cross the lines!**

7. Now draw notes in all the **spaces** of the staff below by drawing circle around the dots. The first two notes are drawn as examples.

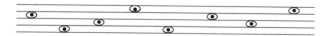

8. Notes drawn correctly on the **spaces** of the staff **fill the space without crossing the lines.** Draw an **X** on all the space notes drawn **incorrectly** on the staff below.

EXPLORE Have fun with your imagination! Draw something that will remind you of notes written on a line or **space.**

LINE NOTE	YOUR PICTURE	SPACE NOTE	YOUR PICTURE
⊕		⊖	

WP350

UNIT 1
LESSON 1
LINES AND SPACES ON THE STAFF

OBJECTIVES
- To understand the difference between a line and a space.
- To understand the construction of the staff = 5 lines and 4 spaces.
- To draw notes carefully on lines and spaces.
- To recognize notes that are drawn incorrectly on lines and spaces.

TEACHING TIPS
- When young students are asked to write "on the line" in their classrooms it looks like this:

  Susie Smith

  In music, writing "on the line" looks like this: ~~Susie Smith~~ Keep this in mind when introducing staff **lines** and **spaces**. The concept can be confusing at first, so lots of visual examples such as the apple (line) and the belt buckle (space) may be helpful. Ask your students for more ideas!

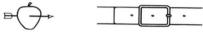

- Accurate placement of notes on lines and spaces is an essential starting point for music theory. Emphasize writing **large** notes **around** the line (a line note) or **between** the lines (a space note). Young students often write tiny notes all crammed together. From the first lesson stress that there should be some "air" between notes.

- Enlarge EXPLORE drawings to create posters to share student perceptions of line and space notes

EXTEND Use Student pages 28-29 (Extend segments are suggestions to use with students who need, or feel more secure with, "reinforcements.")
- Discover objects that are within a "space" or on a "line" in the classroom or at home. Share ideas and draw.
- Draw dots on lines and spaces and practice writing notes around the dots. You may also do this on notebook paper.

EXCEL Use Student pages 28-29 (Excel segments are suggestions to use with students who can "go beyond" the basic lesson.)

- Discover **up and down** and **skips and steps** by drawing notes around dots drawn on:

- lines: going UP; going DOWN
- spaces: going UP; going DOWN
- lines and spaces: going UP
- lines and spaces: going DOWN

LESSON 2
TREBLE AND BASS CLEFS

OBJECTIVES
• To understand that the treble staff shows high pitches.
• To understand that the bass staff shows low pitches.
• To write the clefs on the staff.

TEACHING TIPS
Treble clef: Extra drill may be necessary to draw this accurately. This step-by-step approach is most successful: First draw the long line down. At the top, make a narrow D that stops at the **2nd line from the top** (presented as the D line in the next lesson), then make a big G that wraps around the **2nd line from the bottom**. The G line must be crossed three times. **Bass clef:** Accuracy relies on placement of the dots—the first is on the **2nd line from the top**, and the others are **above and below** this line. The other part is like the right half of a heart which stops just below the **2nd line from the bottom**.
C clef: Students who play C clef instruments can practice drawing that clef sign on pages 28 and 29. C clef headings in this book give tips to these students. Students who play tenor clef or other C clefs may adjust examples accordingly.

EXTEND Use Student pages 28-29
• Before drawing a treble clef or bass clef, draw dots on the **second lines** to use as guidelines.

EXCEL
• Are there any other clefs? (What clef is for violas?)
• What did these clefs look like long ago?

EXPLORE
OBJECTIVES
• Link instruments and their ranges with clefs learned.
• Understand concepts of high and low.
• Introduce grand staff and instruments that use it.
• Introduce sound (timbre) and pitch of different instruments. This is the first Listening example. indicates the cassette is needed. Stop the cassette when the bell is heard at the end of each example. The excerpts are from:
  A. Boccherini: *Minuet in A* (violin)
  B. Rameau: *Gavotte et Doubles from Nouvelles Suites de Pieces de Clavecin* (harpsichord)
  C. Schubert: *Symphony No.9, 1st movement* (trombone)
Students may easily use the cassettes at home; all of the directions are clearly announced along with page numbers. If parents wish to assist, answers are on page 64.

EXTEND
• Make movements reflecting high and low sounds of orchestral instruments. There are many opportunities in Britten's *The Young Person's Guide to the Orchestra* and Saint-Saëns' *Carnival of the Animals*.

EXCEL
• Listen to performances by students, if possible, who play different instruments and can explain the range and clef.
• Explore other instruments that use the grand staff.
• Listen to other harpsichord recordings and discuss the instrument.
• What does a conductor use as a staff? Explore a full score!

6

LESSON
2

TREBLE AND BASS CLEFS

The **TREBLE CLEF** is written on the staff that shows notes that are **HIGH** in pitch. The bracket over the piano keyboard below shows the keys that have notes written in the **TREBLE STAFF**.

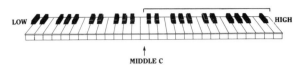

MIDDLE C

1. The treble clef is drawn around the **second line up from the BOTTOM** of the staff. Follow the steps below, tracing the dotted lines and drawing **treble clefs**.

1.   2.   3.   TRACE   YOUR TURN

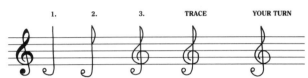

The **BASS CLEF** is drawn on the staff that shows notes that are **LOW** in pitch. The bracket over the piano keyboard below shows the keys that have notes written in the **BASS STAFF**.

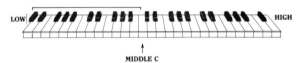

MIDDLE C

2. The bass clef is drawn around **the second line from the TOP** of the staff. Follow the steps below, tracing the lines and drawing **bass clefs**.

1.   2.   3.   TRACE   YOUR TURN

WP350

EXPLORE

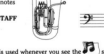 The notes written in the **TREBLE STAFF** and the **BASS STAFF** describe sounds of many instruments as well as sounds we sing. Keyboard instruments such as the piano, organ, or synthesizer use the treble staff and bass staff together to make a **GRAND STAFF**:

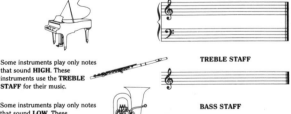

Some instruments play only notes that sound **HIGH**. These instruments use the **TREBLE STAFF** for their music.

TREBLE STAFF

Some instruments play only notes that sound **LOW**. These instruments use the **BASS STAFF** for their music.

BASS STAFF

The **EXPLORATIONS** tape is used whenever you see the symbol on the page. Listen to the tape for examples of sounds of different instruments that play **high** notes, **low** notes, and the full range from **high** to **low**.

1. Circle the **staff** you think would be used for the instruments you hear.

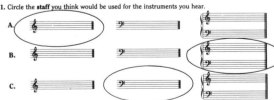

EXPLORE BONUS Which instruments did you hear on the tape? Write the correct letter names beside the pictures.

A ___ ___ B ___ C ___ ___

WP350

8

LESSON 3
LETTER NAMES ON THE STAFF

Each note written on the staff has a name that is a letter of the **MUSIC ALPHABET.** This alphabet uses only the letters A B C D E F G, repeating as the notes go up the staff.

1. The **treble staff** below shows all the notes on the staff. Fill in the missing letters using the music alphabet—A B C D E F G A B C D E F G.

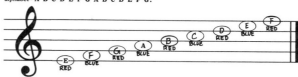

2. Color all the notes written on **lines** on the **treble staff** red.

The names of the **treble staff lines** are E G B D F .

3. Color all the notes written on **spaces** on the **treble staff** blue.

The names of the **treble staff spaces** are F A C E .

4. The **bass staff** below shows all the notes on the staff. Fill in the missing letters using the music alphabet—A B C D E F G A B C D E F G.

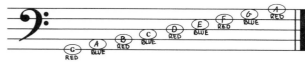

5. Color all the notes written on **lines** on the bass staff red.

The names of the **bass staff lines** are G B D F A .

6. Color all the notes written on **spaces** on the bass staff blue.

The names of the **bass staff spaces** are A C E G .

WP350

9

NOTES ON THE STAFF

Now you are ready to discover how the **lines** and **spaces**, **treble** and **bass clefs**, and **letter names** you have learned work together to write notes on the staff correctly.

1. A. Draw a **treble clef** on the empty staff below.
   B. Draw notes on each **line** on the staff, going from bottom to top.
   C. Write the correct **letter name** for each note inside the note as shown.
   (You discovered these letter names on page 8, number 2.)

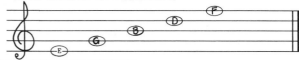

2. A. Draw a **treble clef** on the empty staff below.
   B. Draw notes on each **space** on the staff, going from bottom to top.
   C. Write the correct **letter name** for each note inside the note as shown.
   (You discovered these letter names on page 8, number 3.)

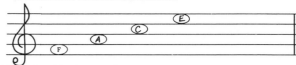

3. A. Draw a **bass clef** on the empty staff below.
   B. Draw notes on each **line** on the staff, going from bottom to top.
   C. Write the correct **letter name** for each note inside the note as shown.
   (You discovered these letter names on page 8, number 5.)

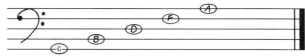

4. A. Draw a **bass clef** on the empty staff below.
   B. Draw notes on each **space** on the staff, going from bottom to top.
   C. Write the correct **letter name** for each note inside the note as shown.
   (You discovered these letter names on page 8, number 6.)

WP350

LESSON 3
LETTER NAMES ON THE STAFF

OBJECTIVES
• To understand the music alphabet.
• To discover the note names of the spaces on the treble and bass staffs.
• To discover the note names of the lines on the treble and bass staffs.

TEACHING TIPS
• It is sometimes hard for students to remember to stop at G for the music alphabet since they are accustomed to using the complete alphabet. Introduce the lesson with a bit of alphabet fun. Ask students to write A B C D E F G three times in a row to get used to the repeating pattern.
• Coloring the notes allows students to <u>discover</u> the letter names, rather than learning by rote. As they color, students will also make the visual connection of skipping lines and spaces on the staff.
C clef: Use pages 28-29 to practice letter names on any C staff. See example below.

EXTEND Use blank or lined paper
• Write the music alphabet. Use red and blue pencils to circle every other letter to show the letter names of lines and spaces.

EXCEL Use Student pages 28-29
• Write the notes going **down** the staff. Color the line and space notes with two different colors. Write the letters in **backward** order.

NOTES ON THE STAFF

OBJECTIVES
• To write note letter names on the staff.
• To reinforce writing notes on lines and spaces.
• To reinforce drawing treble and bass clef signs.

TEACHING TIPS
• Look for "a pencil point of air" between notes (instead of being crammed together) written on the staff and notes **exactly** on lines and spaces. Also, are clefs written on and around the second lines?
• By coloring notes on the staff, students apply what they have learned and make connections between notes, clefs, staff, and letter names. They put it all together through discovery and analysis.
C clef: Use pages 28-29 or the back of the Student Book to practice writing space and line notes.

EXTEND
• A Practice Page follows this lesson.

EXCEL *Use Student pages 28-29*
• Write the line letter names going **down** each staff.
• Write the space letter names going **down** each staff.

PRACTICE PAGE

TEACHING TIPS
• Both of the E's and F's in the treble staff and G's and A's in the bass staff are acceptable for writing music words.

EXTEND Use Student pages 28-29
• Write notes and letter names on the treble staff and bass staff.
• Write clef signs.

EXCEL Use Student pages 28-29
• Discover notes above or below the staff from what you already know!

EXPLORE
OBJECTIVES
• To apply writing notes and letter names in a creative activity.
• To encourage creative answers that require a synthesis of what has been learned.

TEACHING TIPS
• The words listed on the page are suggestions that may be used along with the many words students will create.
• Suggest the first letters of words, "words that begin with B," with a few examples to get students started. Accept correct notes written above and below the staff (see EXCEL above). Make a large list of students' words and keep it posted as an excellent visual aid for the upcoming LESSON 4.

List some of the words your students created for future reference:

_____   _____
_____   _____
_____   _____

C clef: Have students draw a C clef on the bottom staff and create their words.

EXTEND
• Use the music words written on page 10 to get ideas for more words!

EXCEL
• Bonus for those who make words longer than four letters.
• Bonus for those who create the longest list of words.

PRACTICE PAGE

TREBLE STAFF LINES   TREBLE STAFF SPACES

1. Write the correct letter names below the notes written on this **treble staff**. They should spell words.

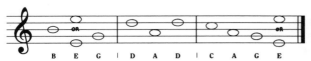

B   E   D | F   A   C   E | C   A   B

2. Draw the notes on the **treble staff** using lines or spaces to fit the words.

B   E   G | D   A   D | C   A   G   E

BASS STAFF LINES   BASS STAFF SPACES

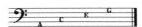

3. Write the correct letter names below the notes written on this **bass staff**. They should spell words.

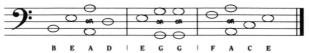

C   A   B   B   A   G   E | D   E   E   D

4. Draw the notes on the **bass staff** using lines or spaces to fit the words below.

B   E   A   D | E   G   G | F   A   C   E

EXPLORE

It is fun to make up **your own** music words using the notes on the staff.

1. The music alphabet is shown below. Make up words using only these letters and write them on the lines below. The first word is given as an example.

A B C D E F G

My music words:

FEED	CABBAGE	BEEF
BEAD	BAGGAGE	EGG
BAG	CAGE	EDGE

2. Draw a **treble clef** on the staff below. Choose three words from your list and draw them on the treble staff using notes on the lines and spaces you have learned.

My music words: A C E   B A D   A B E

3. Draw a **bass clef** on the staff below. Choose three words from your list and draw them on the bass staff using notes on the lines and spaces you have learned.

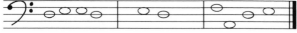

My music words: DE ED   E D   FADE

Use the staff below for extra music words you have discovered.

_____
_____
_____

12

LESSON 4
MUSIC STORIES

A different way to practice the letter names on the staff is to work on a **MUSIC STORY.**
1. Fill in the letter names of the music words in the following story.

A TRIP TO THE FARM

Once upon [A] time. [E D] and [A B E] went to the farm.

They enjoyed finding [E G G] s and picking [CABBAGE] s.

[A B E] was stung by a [B E E] ! " Ouch!" said [A B E]

They went to [F E E D] the pigs. Then they packed their [BAGGAGE]

and went home.

2. Now it is your turn to create your own **music story.** First, copy below the music words you discovered on page 11.

_____
_____

3. Now use your imagination and write a story connecting as many of the words from the list above into your story. Underline the music words.

_____
_____
_____
_____

WP350

13

Write your music story below, using the manuscript paper to write the notes on the staff that spell your music words. Put in blanks for letter names under each note. Let your friends try to write the letter names of **your** music story! Draw a picture above your story.

Title: _____
By: _____ Date: _____

EXPLORE Write another music story on page 59.

WP350

LESSON 4
MUSIC STORIES

OBJECTIVES
· To reinforce the letter names of notes on treble and bass staffs through a creative activity.
· To develop a creative product from what has been learned.

TEACHING TIPS
· Encourage students to write stories at least **three** sentences long using at least five "music words." The story can be written along the top of the staff, with music words notated on the staff. Each music word should have blanks written beneath each note.
· Photocopy each student's music story and give to other students to complete—an enjoyable way to drill letter names!
C clef: Include the C clef words created on page 11 in your music story.

EXTEND
· Practice note names and staff placement with flashcards (make your own or use *Bastien Music Flashcards* published by Neil A. Kjos Music Company).
· Use 3 by 5 cards to create music word flash cards. Draw notes that spell a word on a staff on one side and write the matching word on the back.

EXCEL Use Student page 59
· Why stop at only one story? There's room for more!

**LESSON 5
NOTES IN RHYTHMS**

OBJECTIVES
• To learn the rhythmic feel of quarter notes and half notes through clapping while saying syllables and words.
• To write quarter notes and half notes accurately.
• To learn the structure of measures and bar lines.

TEACHING TIPS
• The steady pulse of the quarter note can be felt with ease if clapping is a circular gesture with hands released upward after each clap, rather than "stopped" when hands come together. The "bob" is done with a closed hand gesturing forward and down with a circular motion. The "bob" emphasizes holding the note for the "bob" of a second beat.
• The tape sets the tempo for $\frac{4}{4}$ by saying "ready to clap and."
• Ideally, do 2 with the student to initiate good rhythmic reading. Eyes need to work in tandem with the ears! Do students end <u>exactly</u> with the tape?
• Emphasize that noteheads need to be an oval, not a circle, with upright stems on the **right** side. Suggest filling in quarter notes with steady circular strokes instead of going back and forth. It's quicker!

EXTEND
• Get into two groups: one clapping ♩ and one clapping ♩. Make **large** bobbing gestures for the notes! Use a conductor to keep groups together.
• Draw quarter notes in a space and half notes on a line.

EXCEL Use Student page 29
• Create another rhythm excercise using CLAP and STAMP.
• Add words to fit your new rhythms and perform for others.
• Create rhythm patterns using ♩♩. What words will fit your new rhythm patterns?
Example:

Ice-cream cone   Blue   shoe

For additional creative ideas with rhythm, movement, and words, refer to *Rhythm Antics* by Joanne Haroutounian, published by the Neil A. Kjos Music Company.

14

LESSON 5

NOTES IN RHYTHMS

Now that you have put notes onto the staff correctly, you can learn to fit these notes to the **RHYTHM** of music. **Rhythm** is based on the natural beat of music.

QUARTER NOTE = 1 BEAT   ♩ = 1 BEAT

The rhythm below shows **QUARTER NOTES** in groups of 4 beats in **MEASURES** separated by **BAR LINES** and ending with a **DOUBLE BAR**.

 1. Clap the rhythm below while listening to the **EXPLORATIONS** tape. Say "ta" with each **quarter note** as you clap.

You say: ta ta ta ta   ta ta ta ta   ta ta ta ta

Did you end exactly with the tape?

 2. Draw **quarter** notes on the line below as shown. Be careful to draw the **STEM** on the **right** side of the **NOTEHEAD**.

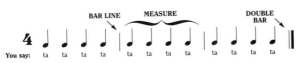

STEM

NOTEHEAD

15

HALF NOTE = 2 BEATS   ♩ = 2 BEATS

A **HALF NOTE** holds for **2 beats**. When clapping rhythms with a **half note**, say the word "half-note" as you clap. The sign means you hold your hands and bob them to the beat to show the second beat.

 3. Clap the rhythm below while listening to the **EXPLORATIONS** tape.

You say: half - note half - note ta ta half - note half - note half - note
You: clap - bob   clap - bob   clap clap clap - bob   clap - bob   clap - bob

 4. Draw **half notes** in the space between the lines below as shown. Watch for proper **stems**.

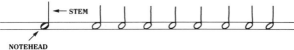

← STEM

NOTEHEAD

5. The rhythm exercise below lets you clap and stamp to ♩ and ♩. Try it!

CLAP
STAMP

 EXPLORE Write your own rhythm using ♩ and ♩ below. Each measure should have 4 beats.

Now draw your rhythm on the two-line staff below, creating a rhythm exercise to enjoy.

CLAP
STAMP

16

A RHYTHM WORKOUT

1. **Clap** with the metronome and say the words or syllables **out loud.**
2. **Clap** with the metronome and "think" the words or syllables.
3. Keep the steady beat "inside" with no metronome and "think" the words or syllables while clapping the rhythms.
4. **Step** the steady beat while clapping and listening to the rhythms on the **EXPLORATIONS** tape—a final check to your workout!

Metronome: 1 beat = 80

A.

ta ta half-note   half-note half-note ta ta ta ta   ta ta half-note

B.

C.

D.

EXPLORE Share this **Rhythm Workout** with several friends.
1. One person can clap rhythm A while another steps to rhythm B.
2. One person can tap legs (patschen) to rhythm C while another snaps fingers to rhythm D.
3. A **super challenge**—all rhythms together with these rhythm sounds!

WP350

A RHYTHM WORKOUT

OBJECTIVES
• To practice feeling the inner rhythmic pulse of ♩ and ♩.
• To learn to use the metronome while clapping rhythms.
• To physically coordinate a steady pulse and rhythms by stamping and clapping.

TEACHING TIPS
• If a metronome is not available, tap rhythm sticks or on a table to create a sound that differs from clapping or stamping. Emphasizing different rhythm sounds promotes a keen perception of rhythmic differences, and adds a bit of fun!
• This page is excellent for classes. Use the four rhythms with different sounds as suggested in EXPLORE.

EXTEND
• Draw the "bob" mark (⌢) below each half note.
• Begin the rhythms at a slower metronome mark and work up to 80.

EXCEL Use Student page 29
• Add words to match the rhythm patterns.
• Place two of these exercises on a two-line rhythm staff. Perform with two people or two groups, listening to the different rhythm sounds.

17

LESSON 6

MORE NOTES AND A REST

DOTTED HALF NOTE = 3 BEATS   ♩. = 3 BEATS

The **DOTTED HALF NOTE** holds for 3 beats. When clapping rhythms with a dotted half note, you can say "**half-note-dot**" to each note, clapping and bobbing as shown.

1. Clap the rhythms below while listening to the **EXPLORATIONS** tape.

3
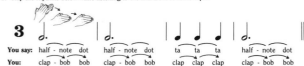

You say: half - note dot   half - note dot   ta   ta   ta   half - note dot
You: clap - bob bob   clap - bob bob   clap clap clap   clap - bob bob

2. Draw **dotted half notes** on the line below as shown. Draw the proper placement of the **stem** and **notehead** and don't forget the **dot**!

3. The rhythms below are in groups of 4 beats and 3 beats. Try another **Rhythm Workout** with these rhythms using the directions given on page 16. Check your workout with the **EXPLORATIONS** tape.

Metronome: 1 beat = 80

A.
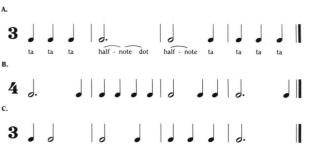
ta ta ta   half - note dot   half - note   ta   ta   ta   ta

B.
4

C.
3

WP350

LESSON 6
MORE NOTES AND A REST

OBJECTIVES
• To learn the rhythmic feel of a dotted half note, whole note, and quarter rest through clapping while saying syllables and words.
• To write dotted half notes, whole notes, and quarter rests accurately.
• To clap and step to all the rhythms learned in many combinations.
• To write these notes and rests in measures of three and four beats.

TEACHING TIP
• The RHYTHM WORKOUT directions on page 16 should be followed in number 3. Use ♫6 as a **final** check **after** students have worked through the workout themselves.

TEACHING TIPS
Rhythm exercises:
• Each note is introduced by using it with clapping and saying syllables. Saying words and syllables out loud while clapping will ease any confusion about holding these notes properly. Exaggerate the "bob" of the held beats for real success in holding ♩ , ♩. , and 𝅝 for the exact amount of beats.

• The quarter rest requires hands to be circled out and "open" with a definite bob of a beat and a whispered "rest." If students keep a very quiet "rest" in the exercises, it adds variety of sound and emphasizes silence in rhythm.

• The RHYTHM WORKOUT directions on page 16 should be followed in number 8. Use 9 as a **final** check **after** students have worked through the workout themselves.

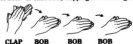

WHOLE NOTE - 4 BEATS   𝅝 - 4 BEATS

The **WHOLE NOTE holds for 4 beats.** When clapping rhythms with a whole note, you can say the words **"hold-that-whole-note"** to each note, clapping and bobbing as shown below.

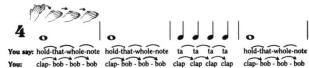

CLAP   BOB   BOB   BOB

4. Clap the rhythms below while listening to the **EXPLORATIONS** tape.

You say: hold-that-whole-note hold-that-whole-note ta ta ta ta hold-that-whole-note
You: clap- bob - bob - bob   clap- bob - bob - bob   clap clap clap clap   clap- bob - bob - bob

5. Draw **whole notes** in the space between the lines below as shown.

QUARTER REST - 1 BEAT   𝄽 - 1 BEAT

The **QUARTER REST shows one beat of REST**. When you see a **quarter rest** in rhythms, you can say the word "rest" in a whisper with your hands apart and NOT clapping. Rests show us silence in the music.

"REST"

6. Clap the following while listening to the **EXPLORATIONS** tape:

3 ♩ ♩ 𝄽 | ♩ ♩ 𝄽 | ♩ ♩ ♩ | 𝄽 ♩ 𝄽 ‖

You say: ta   ta   "rest"   ta   ta   "rest"   ta   ta   ta   "rest" ta "rest"
You: clap clap open   clap clap open   clap clap clap   open clap open

WP350

TEACHING TIPS
Drawing notes and rests:
• Be sure students know that the dot goes above the line when writing a dotted half note on a line.

• Students may need extra drill in writing the quarter rest accurately.

• Emphasize clear-cut angles in drawing a rest.

EXTEND Use Student pages 28-29
• Draw dotted half notes on a space and whole notes on a line.

• Practice writing extra rhythm examples using all the notes you have learned.

EXCEL Use Student page 29
• Perform the RHYTHM WORKOUT in number 8 at metronome = 92 and then 100!

• Write the rhythms created in **Explore** on a two-line rhythm staff and have them performed.

7. Draw **quarter rests** on the full staff below as shown.

TRACE   YOUR TURN

8. Putting it together! Clap the following rhythms below that combine ♩ ♩ ♩. 𝅝 𝄽. Use the **Rhythm Workout** ideas you have learned. Check your workout with the **EXPLORATIONS** tape.

A.
4 ♩ ♩ ♩ 𝄽 | ♩. ♩ ♩ | ♩ ♩ | 𝅝 ‖

ta ta ta "rest" half - note dot ta half - note ta ta hold that whole note

B.
3 ♩ ♩ 𝄽 | ♩ 𝄽 ♩ | ♩ ♩ | ♩. ‖

C.
4 ♩ ♩ ♩ ♩ | 𝄽 𝄽 ♩ ♩ | ♩. ♩ | 𝅝 ‖

D.
3 ♩ ♩ | ♩. | 𝄽 ♩ ♩ | ♩. ‖

How did you do on this rhythm challenge?

SUPER JOB ☐   DOING O.K. ☐   NEED MORE WORK ☐

EXPLORE Your turn! Write your own rhythms below using ♩ ♩ ♩. 𝅝 𝄽

Remember: **4** - 4 beats in each measure   **3** - 3 beats in each measure

A.
3 | | | ‖

B.
4 | | | ‖

20

LESSON 7

TIME SIGNATURES

The **TIME SIGNATURE** shows how many beats are in each measure in the music. You have clapped to groups of 4 beats and groups of 3 beats. The proper way of showing this in music is:

$\frac{4}{4}$ 4 BEATS IN EACH MEASURE
  QUARTER NOTE ♩ = 1 BEAT

The TOP number tells how many beats are in each measure.
The BOTTOM number tells what kind of note = 1 beat. (4 = ♩)

1. Fill in the line that explains the **time signature** written below, using the rule above as a clue.

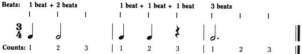

$\frac{3}{4}$ _3 beats in each measure_
  QUARTER NOTE ♩ = 1 BEAT

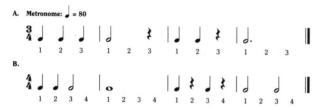

2. Clap the rhythms below **three ways:**

1. "Think" the words and syllables you have learned as you clap.
2. Count the numbers below the measures **out loud** as you clap.
3. "Think" the numbers below the measures as you clap.

Check your work with the **EXPLORATIONS** tape

A. Metronome: ♩ = 80

B.

21

3. Write the counts below each measure to match the **time signatures** given.

4. Discover the correct **time signature** of the measures below:

If the counts = 3 beats, draw a $\frac{3}{4}$.   If the counts = 4 beats, draw a $\frac{4}{4}$.

To discover the correct **time signature:**
1. Write the counts below each measure. This will let you discover how many beats are in each measure.
2. Place the correct time signature in the boxes.

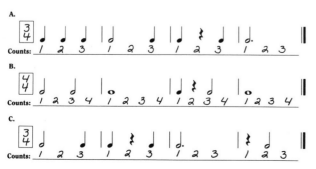

WP350

LESSON 7
TIME SIGNATURES

OBJECTIVES
• To understand the meaning of $\frac{4}{4}$ and $\frac{3}{4}$.
• To apply the different notes and rest learned through clapping and writing counts below $\frac{3}{4}$ and $\frac{4}{4}$ measures.
• To discover the time signature from the number of counts in measures.

TEACHING TIPS
• Introduce the lesson with a clear-cut explanation of the meaning of the TOP number and the BOTTOM number of the time signature. By filling in the line that explains the number of counts, students discover the difference between $\frac{4}{4}$ and $\frac{3}{4}$.
• The step-by-step directions under number 2 should ease students from clapping with words and syllables to clapping the "counts" in each measure. Emphasize a full voice when counting out loud. Use the EXPLORATIONS IN MUSIC cassette ♫ 10 as a **final** check after students work through the counting themselves.

TEACHING TIPS
• In number 4, be sure students write the counts below the measures **first**, then write the time signature. This step-wise approach allows them to discover the key signature with success.

EXTEND
• A Practice Page follows this lesson on page 22.

EXCEL
• What do the time signatures of $\frac{2}{4}$ and $\frac{5}{4}$ mean?
• For a "Rhythm Olympics" idea refer to *Rhythm Antics* by Joanne Haroutounian, published by the Neil A. Kjos Music Company.

PRACTICE PAGE

TEACHING TIPS
• Students can complete the measures in number 1 in a number of ways. The answer page shows two possibilities, but any combination that equals the missing beats is correct.
• Students can show they understand the connection of beats, note values, and time signatures when filling in empty measures (number 4). Check this example carefully to identify students who may need extra help.
• Several students, or groups, may want to perform the rhythm exercise they create in EXPLORE. Try two or three groups performing different exercises at once!

EXTEND Use Student page 29
• Create additional practice in filling in measures with notes and rests.
• Add motions and words to your creations.

EXCEL Use Student page 29
• Write rhythms with new time signatures of $\frac{2}{4}$ and $\frac{5}{4}$!
• Add motions and words to your creations.

22

PRACTICE PAGE

You can have fun solving a few problems on this Practice Page. Each example has a different problem that needs your help. Good Luck!

1. Help! The measures below are missing notes and we need your help to **fill each measure to match the correct number of beats with** ♩ ♩ ♩ . ◦ . The **time signatures** will give you a musical clue.

2. Another problem! The measures below are missing the counts below each measure. **Write the correct counts**, looking at the **time signature** and notes in each measure.

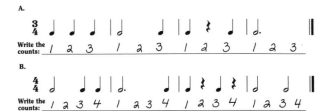

23

3. Now the measures are missing **bar lines** and **double bars** at the end! To solve this problem you must:
A. Look at the **time signature** to see how many beats are in each measure.
B. Write the counts below each measure.
C. Draw the bar lines as you discover each full measure and end with a double bar.

A.

$\frac{3}{4}$

Write the counts: 1 2 3   1 2 3   1 2 3   1 2 3

B.

$\frac{4}{4}$

Write the counts: 1 2 3 4 1 2 3 4 1 2 3 4 1 2 3 4

4. A real problem—empty measures! **Your** job is to fill them properly with notes and rests and write counts below each measure. Thank you!

A.

$\frac{3}{4}$

Write the counts: _____

B.

$\frac{4}{4}$

Write the counts: _____

EXPLORE A reward for your difficult task! The two-line rhythm staff below uses a rhythm with clapping and stamping as shown. It's fun to do—try it!

CLAP $\frac{3}{4}$

STAMP

EXPLORE BONUS Your turn to create a rhythm exercise below.

CLAP $\frac{3}{4}$

STAMP

24

LESSON 8

LISTEN, AND CREATE RHYTHMS

You are ready to listen to rhythms like a **MUSICAL DETECTIVE!**

11

1. Listen to the **EXPLORATIONS** tape for rhythms that may be the **SAME** or **DIFFERENT** from the rhythms written below. Circle the correct answer.

Rhythms have a natural **ACCENT** or stronger beat on the first beat of the measure.

2. Listen to the following examples on the **EXPLORATIONS** tape.

3. Listen to the **EXPLORATIONS** tape for examples of rhythms in 4/4 and 3/4. Circle what you hear.

A. ④/④ ③/④   C. ④/④ ③/④

B. ④/④ ③/④   D. ④/④ ③/④

WP350

25

4. Just for fun, get up and move around to some rhythm exercises. In the exercises below, do the following movements to each note or rest:

STEP   TOUCH HEAD   TOUCH TOES   STRETCH HIGH

Metronome: Try three different ways: **SLOW** ♩ = 76   **MEDIUM** ♩ = 92   **FAST** ♩ = 108

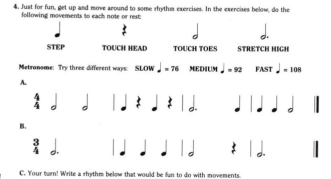

C. Your turn! Write a rhythm below that would be fun to do with movements.

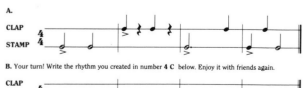

5. The rhythm from number 4 A is written below on a two-line rhythm staff. Share the fun with a friend or your teacher. One person or group can do the movements to 4 A and the other can do 5 A. Add **accents** for extra interest. Take the challenge!

A.

B. Your turn! Write the rhythm you created in number 4 C below. Enjoy it with friends again.

CLAP 4/4
STAMP 4/4

EXPLORE Can you think of new movements to use to describe the notes and rest below? Try the exercises above with **your** movements.

WP350

LESSON 8
LISTEN, AND CREATE RHYTHMS

OBJECTIVES
- To identify written rhythms learned through listening.
- To learn about accented beats in 3/4 and 4/4.
- To perceive the difference between 3/4 and 4/4 by listening.
- To reinforce learning rhythms through movement.
- To create rhythm exercises with movement.

TEACHING TIPS
Listen: This lesson encourages students to make connections between what they see and what they hear ("eyes and ears"), to expand their comprehension through listening.

- Before listening to the cassette 🎵 11, it may be wise to review the beats in 3/4 and 4/4 by giving exaggerated **accents** to the first beat of each measure. The Listening Example Answers are on page 62 of the Student Book. Check that students do not refer to it until after they have written their personal decisions.

- This lesson affords a wonderful opportunity to have students become conductors. Demonstrate the conducting patterns for 3/4 and 4/4.

- Repetition of the taped examples may be wise because of the difficulty of identifying time signatures. A follow-up lesson could include listening to the full performance of the listening examples (see titles below) or additional 3/4 and 4/4 compositions of your choice.

- Listening examples used to identify 3/4 and 4/4:
  A. Clementi: *Sonatina op. 36 no. 1* 1st movement (piano)
  B. Mozart: *German Dance K.605 No. 2* (strings)
  C. Klengel: *Kindertrio in G op. 39 no. 2* (piano, violin, cello) from *Chamber Music Sampler, Book 2* Joanne Haroutounian, Editor, Neil A. Kjos Music Company
  D. Haydn: *Symphony No. 48* Menuetto (orchestra)

Create: Ask students for ideas to explore creative movements to match the rhythms. Several groups might perform together doing different things:
- clap-stamp exercise
- movement to rhythms
- rhythm instruments
- see-sawing open fifths on a keyboard or Orff instrument

- Students may create extra Rhythm Exercises on notebook paper: make a column on the left for Rhythm Sounds. Remind students to draw a large time signature to "fit" the rhythm lines. Rhythms can be written on the notebook spaces. The last step is to write words below the rhythms.

EXTEND Use Student page 29 (or notebook paper)
- Decide on a time signature and then draw rhythms in "open" (no staff) measures and on a two-line staff.

EXCEL Use Student page 29 (or notebook paper)
- Write a full rhythm orchestra of sounds and movements: combine two or three rhythm exercises with different rhythm sounds, movements, and words. When you perform this, have a conductor to keep things together!

EXPLORE

OBJECTIVES
· To learn how to analyze music for details.
· To reinforce comprehension of note letter names, rhythms, and time signatures by locating them in the music score.

TEACHING TIPS
· This lesson makes the connection between multiple concepts presented and a music score. This is just a stepping stone away from making the same connection in music learned in lessons.
· Transfer the idea of similar patterns (numbers 5 and 6) from music into everyday experiences by asking students to find visual patterns in a room.
· Students enjoy creating repeated patterns by improvising with rhythms or on their instruments. Do encourage this musical exploration!
· Eager investigators will immediately locate the "new" notes (C, D) in this music score. What better way to introduce these notes than by students discovering them through analysis? (They will be fully presented in EXPLORATIONS IN MUSIC, Book 2.)
New notes:

EXTEND
· Put letter names of all the notes you know above and below the notes of the staff. Circle the notes you do not know.

EXCEL Use Student pages 28-29
· Write the music example in the **bass staff,** starting on second space C and following the same step and skip pattern. Is your new music example higher or lower than what is printed?

BEYOND THE PAGE

OBJECTIVES
· To transfer the concepts learned in EXPLORATIONS IN MUSIC to the music students are learning and performing.
· To teach students how to analyze their own music for details.

TEACHING TIPS
· Follow the format of the Music Investigation Report and ask students to find specific items you select in a piece they are learning.

EXTEND
Use the format of the Music Investigation Report for analysis of melodies that move by step and skip, and repeated melodic patterns.

EXCEL
Use the format of the Music Investigation Report for exploring terms and notes not learned in EXPLORATIONS IN MUSIC. Research your discoveries to find out what they mean!

26

EXPLORE

 You can now explore the music below to find all the musical ideas you have learned.

Polka by Dmitri Kabalevsky (melody only)

 Time to investigate! Look carefully at the musical example above to discover each answer.

1. The time signature for the piece is $\frac{4}{4}$. This tells us that each measure contains ___4___ beats.

The _quarter_ note = 1 beat
(See page 20 for clues.)

2. The piece is written in what staff? Circle: (TREBLE)   BASS   GRAND STAFF

 3. The circled notes have the following letter names:

A. _G_   B. _E_   c. _F_

4. How many half notes can you find in the music?   __6__

5. The following measures have the exact same notes and rhythm:

__1__ and _5_   __2__ and _3_

6. Look at the rhythm written below. Can you find this rhythm pattern in the music? Circle the pattern each time you see it. ♩ ♩ ♩

I found this pattern ___4___ times in the music.

WP350

27

BEYOND THE PAGE

 Now you can look at your own music to discover details about notes on the staff and rhythms that you have learned in **EXPLORATIONS.**

Investigate the music you are learning in lessons for—

1. **Time signature of the piece.** It may be different from $\frac{4}{4}$ or $\frac{3}{4}$.

2. **Letter names of the first note, or notes, in the piece.**
(Include treble and bass staff notes if you play a keyboard instrument)

3. **Repeated rhythm patterns in the piece.** Draw the pattern and write the measure numbers where you found this pattern.

MY MUSICAL INVESTIGATION

Title	Composer	Time sig.	1st note(s)	Rhythm pattern	Where?

Other musical "clues" I discovered in my investigation:

_____

_____

Bravo! EXCELLENT detective work!   WP350

TEST YOUR SKILLS

30
UNIT 1 TEST

_____ *Your Score*

1. Draw a **treble clef** on the staff below. **Draw notes on lines** around the dots shown. **Write the letter names below each of these notes.**   _____ of 13 points

G   D   E   B   F   G

2. Write in the correct letter names below the notes written on the **treble staff** below.   _____ of 8 points

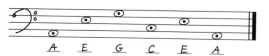

F   B   E   A   D   E   C   G

3. Draw a **bass clef** on the staff below. **Draw notes on spaces** around the dots shown. **Write the letter names below each of these notes.**   _____ of 13 points

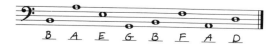

A   E   G   C   E   A

4. Write in the correct letter names below the notes written on the **bass staff** below.   _____ of 8 points

B   A   E   G   B   F   A   D

5. Draw the notes to fit the words below.   _____ of 8 points

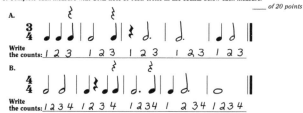

B   E   A   D   C   A   G   E

WP350

31

6. Complete each measure with **ONE note or rest. Write in the counts** below each measure.   _____ of 20 points

A.

Write the counts: 1 2 3   1 2 3   1 2 3   1 2 3   1 2 3

B.

Write the counts: 1 2 3 4   1 2 3 4   1 2 3 4   1 2 3 4   1 2 3 4

7. Draw a line from the symbol or note to the words that describe it below. **Circle the symbol or note that is not connected to words.**   _____ of 8 points

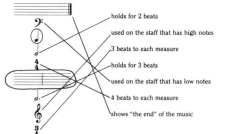

holds for 2 beats

used on the staff that has high notes

3 beats to each measure

holds for 3 beats

used on the staff that has low notes

4 beats to each measure

shows "the end" of the music

8. Draw bar lines and a double bar in the correct places in these examples. Look carefully at the time signatures and **write in the counts** below each measure.   _____ of 14 points

Write the counts: 1 2 3   1 2 3   1 2 3   1   2 3   1 2 3 4   1 2   3 4 1 2 3 4

9. Fill in the measures below with ♩ ♩ ♩ ○ 𝄽 . **Write in the counts** below each measure.   _____ of 8 points

Write the counts:

WP350

PRACTICE PAGE
Pages 28 and 29 are for extra drill and creative work in preparation for TEST YOUR SKILLS for Unit 1.

UNIT 1
TEST YOUR SKILLS

TEACHING TIPS
C clef: Have students draw C clefs for numbers 1 and 3.
Answers for alto clef: 1. A E F C G A   3. G D F B D G
• You may use the Student Progress Chart (inside front cover) to record test scores and make other comments.
Scoring Key:

	POINTS	TOTAL POINTS
1. Each note	1	13
Each letter	1	
Treble clef	1	

There are many details to check with the clefs!

2. Each letter	1	8
3. Each note	1	13
Each letter	1	
Bass clef	1	
4. Each letter	1	8
5. Each note	1	8

---

6. Either a quarter note or rest is correct for these measures.

Each measure note/rest	1	20
Each measure of counts	1	
7. Each match	1	8
Each circle	1	
8. Each bar line/double bar	1	14
Each measure of counts	1	
9. Each measure filled in	1	8
Each measure of counts	1	

TOTAL TEST SCORE: 100 points

UNIT 2
LESSON 9
MELODY SHAPES

OBJECTIVES
• To connect the written melody shape with the sound of the shape.
• To understand melodic movement up and down by steps and skips, visually and aurally.
• To understand repeated notes in a melody visually and aurally.
• To create melody shapes by steps and skips.
• To reinforce the concept of steps and skips on the staff by writing and analyzing melody shapes.

TEACHING TIPS
• Tracing the melody shapes allows students to concentrate on the movement of notes on the staff **as they listen** to the melody shapes on the tape. Watch for careful tracing of the melody that mirrors what they hear, and not a quick line they draw ahead of what they hear.
• Answers written are not the only correct ones! Any shape that shows movement only by step (number 2) and only by skip (number 4) is accurate.
• Melody shapes that include repeated notes can be an outgrowth of this lesson. Staff paper is on Student page 39.
C clef: This clef may be substituted in numbers 2 and 4.
• With the Super Challenge described in EXCEL below, help students with direction of stems. They will learn about it in EXPLORATIONS IN MUSIC, Book 2.
• Encourage students to discover the connection of step/skip of note names on the staff in numbers 5 and 6.

EXTEND Use Student page 39
• Create melody shapes with repeated notes and steps moving up and down.
• Create melody shapes with repeated notes and skips moving up and down.

EXCEL Use Student page 39
• Write melody shapes that combine repeated notes, steps, and skips moving up and down.
• Super challenge! Explore melody shapes that also include rhythm. Follow these steps:
  • Write a treble clef or bass clef on an empty staff.
  • Choose a time signature and write it on the staff.
  • Write rhythms **above** the staff that match your time signature.
  • Use these rhythms in a melody shape using skips, steps, and repeated notes.

Example:
Rhythm:
Melody:

UNIT 2
LESSON 9

MELODY SHAPES

Music is made up of notes that move up and down the staff. This movement makes a shape that is called a **MELODY**. Melodies move by **STEPS** and **SKIPS**.

The **EXPLORATIONS** tape will play the **MELODY SHAPES** below. As you listen, trace the melody with your pencil point. All melodies will be moving by **steps**.

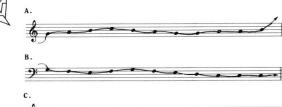

Melody moving UP by STEPS.   Melody moving DOWN by STEPS.

Melody moving UP and DOWN by STEPS.   Melody using REPEATED notes.

1. **Melody shapes:** Listen and trace these melodies that combine the shapes from above.

A.

B.

C.

2. Your turn! Draw a melody shape on the staff below using only steps. The starting note is written. Play this melody on your instrument.

WP350

The melody shapes below move by **skips**. Listen to the **EXPLORATIONS** tape as you trace them with your pencil point.

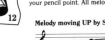

Melody moving UP by SKIPS.   Melody moving DOWN by SKIPS.

Melody moving UP and DOWN by SKIPS.

3. **Melody shapes:** Listen and trace these melodies that combine the shapes from above.

A.

B.

4. Your turn! Draw a melody shape on the staff below using only **skips**. The starting note is written. Play this melody on your instrument.

5. Write the letter names below the following **melody shapes**.

 A. Melody moving UP by STEP.
G A B C D

 B. Melody moving UP by SKIP.
G B D

6. Circle the letters of the music alphabet that match the letters in number 5 A and B.

A. **Steps**
(G) (A) (B) (C) (D) E

B. **Skips**
(G) A (B) C (D) E

34

LESSON 10
LISTEN, AND CREATE MELODIES

It is time to be a Musical Detective for melody shapes!

The **EXPLORATIONS** tape will play three of the **melody shapes** written below.
Before starting the tape, please read these directions!

1. Before listening to the tape, trace the melody shapes with your pencil, singing the shape out loud or "in your head," listening for steps and skips.

2. **Do not trace the melody** when you listen to the tape the first time. Try to hear the melody from the tape "in your head" as you hear it played.

3. Sing the melody you heard out loud or "in your head" and match it to a written melody.

4. Write the correct letter names on the lines.

1. Do you hear A or B? __A__

A. 　　　　　B.

2. Do you hear C or D? __D__

C. 　　　　　D.

3. Do you hear E or F? __E__

E. 　　　　　F.

4. You will hear three notes moving by **step** or by **skip**. Circle what you hear.

A.　(STEP)　SKIP　　　　B.　STEP　(SKIP)

C.　STEP　(SKIP)　　　　D.　(STEP)　SKIP

WP350

35

5. Now it is time for you to be a **COMPOSER!** This page has room for two melody shapes—one using only **steps** and one using only **skips**.

HOW TO COMPOSE MELODY SHAPES
A. Draw the clef that matches your instrument on the empty staff below.
B. Find a note that is comfortable to play as your melody's starting note. Write it on the staff with only a notehead - ●
C. Experiment moving up and down only by **step** on your instrument until you find a melody that sounds interesting. You can repeat notes if you like.
D. **Repeat** this melody over and over until you know it well. Keep it short and simple.
E. Write the notes on the staff.

My **Stepping** Melody Title: _____

6. Follow the same directions to compose a melody shape using only **skips**.

My **Skipping** Melody Title: _____

WP350

LESSON 10
LISTEN, AND CREATE MELODIES

OBJECTIVES
• To introduce sight reading and "inner listening" of written melodies.
• To identify melodic shapes through listening.
• To perceive the difference between the sounds of a step and a skip.
• To apply ideas learned about melodic line to notational skills through composing.
• To understand the creative process of composing and notating melody shapes.

TEACHING TIPS
Listen: One of the most important skills to acquire in music is "inner listening"–hearing the music internally with no "outside" sound. Introduce this lesson by going through each step of the directions on page 34 to secure the practice of this "inner listening" before students listen to the tape.
Create: Students learn to be real composers with this page! Read all directions carefully with the students so that the notation of their melodies will be accurate beginning with their very first "composition." By all means, encourage them to perform their melodies and create new ones.
C clef: Have students write stepping and skipping melodies in the C clef.

EXTEND
• How can you show the movement of melodies that you hear? Experiment by moving with the melody shapes on the tape.
• How can you move by step? By skip? Experiment with your movements as you listen to the steps and skips on the tape.

EXCEL Use Student page 39 or 60
• Compose a melody **question** in the treble staff and a melody **answer** in the bass staff.
　• Does your question melody move up or down?
　• Does your answer melody move up or down?
　• Can you explain why you want them to move this way?

LESSON 11
TRIADS ON C, G, AND F

OBJECTIVES
• To expand the concept of skips into the structure of Major triads built on C, G, and F.
• To draw triads on the lines and spaces of the treble and bass staffs.
• To learn the letter names of these triads.

TEACHING TIPS
• Now that students have written skips in melodies it will be easy to stack them on top of each other to build a triad "snowman." Triad notes should touch the staff lines or each other (depending if on spaces or lines), but without overlapping, and each triad should stand upright on the staff.
• The introduction of Middle C in EXPLORE is linked with its position on the keyboard. Allow students to discover this connection themselves, rather than presenting it to them.
• Students identify triad notes and can see the concept of skips in number 4.
C clef: Assist students in drawing staffs in the open spaces to discover how to draw the C, G, and F triads on the C clef.

C F G

EXTEND
• A PRACTICE PAGE follows this lesson on page 38.

EXCEL Use Student page 39 or 60
• Combine a C Major triad drawn on the bass staff with a melody you create on the treble staff. Begin and end your melody on C.
• Combine a G Major triad drawn on the treble staff with a melody you create on the bass staff. Begin and end your melody on G.

36

TRIADS ON C, G, AND F

TRIADS are formed from 3 notes that are written **skips** apart. You can draw **Major triads** written on C, F, and G from what you have learned. You will learn to write other triads in **EXPLORATIONS IN MUSIC, Book 2.**

To draw **TRIADS** on the staff, think of a **snowman!**

SKIPS →   Triad built on LINES   Triad built on SPACES   ← SKIPS

The triads written below will use a **new note** on the staff.

Notice the note written on its own line: This is **MIDDLE C.**

EXPLORE Why is this note called middle C? Investigate the keyboard pictured on page 6 for clues. Explain your answer to your teacher.

C MAJOR TRIAD

MIDDLE C

1. Write the **C Major** triad below. Be careful that your "snowman" stands straight!

EXPLORE The letter names of these notes are _C_ _E_ and _G_ .

37

F MAJOR TRIAD

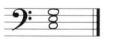

2. Draw the **F Major** triad below.

EXPLORE The letter name of the notes are _F_ _A_ and _C_ .

G MAJOR TRIAD

3. Draw the **G MAJOR TRIAD** below.

EXPLORE The letter names of these notes are _G_ _B_ and _D_ .

4. **Circle the letter names** of the notes in the music alphabet that match the notes in the triads below.

C MAJOR TRIAD	ⓒ	D	ⓔ	F	ⓖ	A	B
F MAJOR TRIAD	Ⓕ	G	Ⓐ	B	ⓒ	D	E
G MAJOR TRIAD	ⓖ	A	Ⓑ	C	Ⓓ	E	F

38

PRACTICE PAGE

1. Write a **melody shape** moving up and down by **step**.

2. Draw the following **triads**.

C MAJOR   F MAJOR   G MAJOR

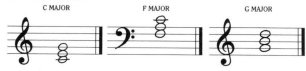

3. Draw a **melody shape** moving up and down by **skip**.

4. Draw a **melody shape** moving by **step** or **skip** using only these notes.

EXPLORE Play the different **triads** you have learned on your instrument. Find the triad that would sound best as an **ACCOMPANIMENT** (harmonies that are background notes) to the melody in number 4. Write it below in the treble staff.

WP350

39

Use the space below for extra drill writing **triads** and **melody shapes** to prepare for **TEST YOUR SKILLS** for **UNIT 2**

WP350

PRACTICE PAGE

OBJECTIVES
• Reinforce writing melody shapes moving up and down by step and skip.
• Reinforce drawing Major triads on C, F, and G.
• Introduce the concept of melody and accompaniment.

TEACHING TIPS
• Melodies written on the answer page are not the only correct melodies. Any melody shape showing the indicated direction is correct.
• Use page 39 for your own ideas for extra drill of writing triads and melody shapes.
C clef: Write the melody shapes in numbers 1, 3, and/or 4 in C clef on page 39.

EXTEND
• Drill, writing C, F, and G triads on both staffs.
• Create additional melody shapes going up and down, with steps, skips, and repeated notes.

EXCEL
• Combine melody shapes with triad accompaniments.
• Write melodies with rhythms.

EXPLORE

OBJECTIVES
• To reinforce the shape of a melodic line through movements.
• To analyze a melody shape within a musical context.
• To introduce dynamics by listening and moving to music.
• To analyze dynamic color in music through listening.

TEACHING TIPS
• This lesson presents a step-by-step process of analysis, from the "ear" to the "eye." Guide the students in tracing the melody line of *Etude*. They may need a second try because the tempo is quite fast.
• The sharp discovered in the "eye" analysis leads to an introduction of half steps and accidentals. EXPLORATIONS IN MUSIC, Book 2 presents these concepts fully.
• Keen investigators will discover new notes (B, A, G♯) written on ledger lines below middle C. Allow them to discover the letter names through their own reasoning rather than by rote.
    New notes:

• Moving to dynamic colors in music fosters keen perception in listening. A follow-up lesson emphasizing movement with other music is an excellent way to reinforce careful listening.

• The curious student will enjoy researching the EXPLORE BONUS about *piano* and *forte*. Have an Italian or good music dictionary handy! A follow-up question—Why are many music terms written in Italian?
• The EXPLORE BONUS example is from Beethoven's *German Dance in G*.
• A wall chart of the EXTEND findings can encourage perceptive listening.
• For additional student exploration of dynamics see "A Day of Dynamics" on page 29 and "A Fantasy Sound Story" on page 30.

EXTEND
• Enjoy the exploration of "A Day of Dynamics."

EXCEL
• Enjoy the exploration of "A Fantasy Sound Story."

40

EXPLORE

The music below shows the melody shape of a piece titled *Etude* by Dmitri Kabalevsky. The rhythm of the notes is not shown.

1. Trace the melody shape **with your fingertip** as you listen to the EXPLORATIONS tape perform this melody shape. **Be careful**—it goes quite fast!

Melody Shape of *Etude* by Dmitri Kabalevsky (opening measures)

WOW! Why not rewind and try it again!

Now answer the questions below investigating what you heard and what you see.

2. The melody shape of *Etude* moved mostly by (circle) (STEPS)   SKIPS

3. The highest note the melody plays has the letter name __A__. It plays __8__ times.

4. There are three **very big skips** in the melody shape. Circle them in the music.

5. Find the new symbol in the music and draw it in the box. **Investigate** this symbol with your teacher.   [#]

6. Draw a box around the **repeated notes** in the music. They have the letter name __A__.

41

LISTENING FOR MUSICAL COLOR

Now you can listen to the *Etude* performed with both the **MELODY** and **ACCOMPANIMENT** (background notes) and with **DYNAMICS**.

DYNAMICS color the music by making it **loud** or **soft** and gradually getting louder and softer.

p	*f*		
soft	loud	gradually getting louder	gradually getting softer
piano	forte	crescendo	decrescendo

BONUS *Piano* and *forte* mean soft and loud in what language? Investigate!

7. Follow the "color path" below **with your eyes** as you listen for **dynamics**.

DYNAMIC COLOR PATH for *Etude* :

8. Now it is time to **move around** to this melody! As the music begins *p*, squat down low making a ball of yourself. As the music ◁ slowly stand up and raise your arms. Reach high overhead when the music reaches *f*. Enjoy this "ear and body" exercise!

Get the tape ready and get into the position for *p*. Begin!

EXPLORE BONUS The **EXPLORATIONS** tape will play another melody and accompaniment for you to discover dynamic color at a slower tempo. Listen and draw your own **dynamic color path** below. Then move around again for another musical "ear and body" exercise!

My dynamic color path:

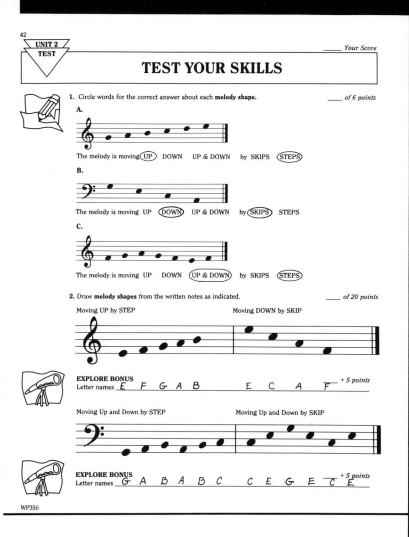

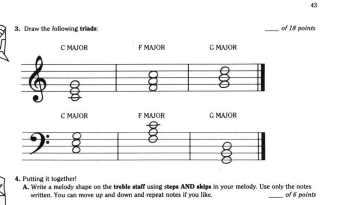

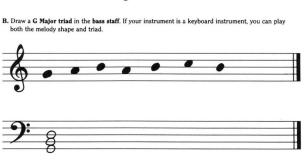

UNIT 2
TEST YOUR SKILLS

C clef: Numbers 2 and 3: Substitute C clef for one or both examples. Number 4: Use the following five-note pattern for students who want to write a melody in C clef.

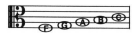

You may record the student test scores and other comments on the **Student Progress Chart** on the inside front cover.

Scoring Key:

	POINTS	TOTAL POINTS
1. Each correct answer	1	6
2. Each melody drawn as described	5	20

The melodies given as answers may be extended. Check that each melody follows the directions.

Explore Bonuses
Each letter, up to 10 — 1 — 10

Bonus is for any 10 notes. Students may have more than 10 notes with letter names for the four melodies. If they do not have 10 letter names correct, count points accordingly.

3. Each note of each triad	1	18
4. Melody as described	4	6
Triad	2	

TOTAL TEST SCORE: 50
TOTAL BONUS SCORE: 10

WP350

WP357

UNIT 3
LESSON 12
LOOK AND LISTEN

OBJECTIVES
• To hear the difference between high and low sounds in music.
• To hear the difference between loud and soft sounds in music.
• To reinforce the concepts of high/low, and loud/soft through drawing.
• To understand the combined concepts of step, skip, and up and down by listening to melody shapes.
• To reinforce the idea of stepping and skipping through drawing.

TEACHING TIPS
• The concepts of **loud and soft** and **high and low** are often confusing to young students. This lesson helps define these qualities through listening and drawing. This aural presentation of steps and skips moving up and down encourages a strong "ear" analysis.
• Students can share what they have drawn with others. Enlargements of these student interpretations will brighten any music room!
• Use page 31 for further exploration of "High & Low, Loud & Soft," and page 32 for "Music Improvisation."
• Music excerpts heard in ♫ 18:
    A. Brahms: *Sonata in E Minor* (cello)
    B. Vivaldi: *Concerto in D Major* (flute)
    C. Mendelssohn: *Concerto in D minor* (violin)

EXTEND
• Enjoy the exploration of "High & Low, Loud & Soft."

EXCEL
• Enjoy the exploration of "Music Improvisation."

---

44 UNIT 3 LESSON 12

LOOK AND LISTEN

You listened for sounds that are **LOW** and **HIGH** when learning about the **treble staff** and the **bass staff**.

LOW SOUNDS   HIGH SOUNDS

You listened for sounds that are **LOUD** and **SOFT** when learning about dynamics.

LOUD SOUNDS   *f*   SOFT SOUNDS   *p*

1. Listen to the **EXPLORATIONS** tape for music that is **high or low** and **loud or soft**. Circle the clef and dynamic signs that describe what you hear.

	HIGH	LOW		LOUD	SOFT
A. The music I heard was	𝄞	(𝄢)	and was	*f*	(*p*)
B. The music I heard was	𝄞	(𝄢)	and was	*f*	(*p*)
C. The music I heard was	𝄞	(𝄢)	and was	(*f*)	*p*

2. Draw something in the box below that would describe a sound that is **low and soft**. Your picture does not have to be about music.

WP350

45

3. Draw something in the box below to describe a sound that is **high and loud**. Your picture does not have to be about music.

4. Listen to the **EXPLORATIONS** tape for notes that are moving **up, down,** or **up and down**. Circle what you hear.

A.	(UP)	DOWN	UP & DOWN
B.	UP	DOWN	(UP & DOWN)
C.	UP	(DOWN)	UP & DOWN
D.	UP	DOWN	(UP & DOWN)

5. Draw something in the boxes below that shows:

STEPPING UP	STEPPING DOWN	SKIPPING UP & DOWN

EXPLORE Try this listening challenge! The **EXPLORATIONS** tape will play notes that are moving by **step** or **skip**. They will be moving **up, down,** or **up and down**.

Listen carefully and circle what you hear. Good luck!

A.	(STEP)	SKIP	moving	(UP)	DOWN	UP & DOWN
B.	STEP	(SKIP)	moving	UP	DOWN	(UP & DOWN)
C.	(STEP)	SKIP	moving	UP	(DOWN)	UP & DOWN

46

EXPLORE

You have learned to listen carefully to melody shapes written on the staff. Now have some fun listening to the shape of melodies by drawing them simply as a line—free and easy!

The **EXPLORATIONS** tape will play several melodies that will be fun to "draw" as you listen to them. The picture below shows a line that might describe the melody on the tape. Listen and see how it shows the movement of what you hear.

MELODY from *Invention in F Major* **by J.S. Bach**

Now it is your turn! Remember there is no "correct" answer. Just listen and draw!

MELODY 1

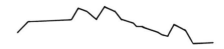

MELODY 2

WP350

LESSON 13
EXPLORE

OBJECTIVES
• To reinforce the idea of melodic movement up and down through listening—not looking at a staff.
• To encourage careful listening for details in the music.
• To create musical lines with a bit more freedom of interpretation.

TEACHING TIPS
• Be sure students have their pencil point near the left margin, with room to go up or down, as the tape begins to play. Encourage them to move the pencil point as they hear the music, "tracking" exactly what they hear. They are tracing the melodic line "with their ears."
• The melody lines shown approximate the melody shapes.
• If students enjoy this activity, at a follow-up lesson use a full piece of drawing paper to "track" the melodic lines they hear. Do not use an example longer than 5-10 seconds long or they will run out of paper!

EXTEND
• Rewind the tape and conduct the music by moving your arms high and low to match the melody line you hear.

EXCEL
• Practice drawing other melodic lines as you listen to music at home.
• Listen only to the very opening words of a favorite song and track the melody line.

47

BEYOND THE PAGE

You can now investigate the music you are learning for all the things you have learned in **EXPLORATIONS IN MUSIC, Book 1.** Choose a piece you enjoy and discover the following:

Title: _____

Composer: _____ Date: _____

1. Copy the first measure of your piece below. Be sure to include the correct **clefs** and **time signature** that are written on each staff.

_____
_____
_____
_____
_____

_____
_____
_____
_____
_____

2. The **time signature** of the piece is: ☐ This means there are _____ beats in each measure and that the

_____ note = 1 beat.

3. Write the letter name under **each note** in the measure above.

4. The **highest** note in the measure has the letter name _____.

5. The **lowest** note in the measure has the letter name _____.

6. Can you find a **step** in the measure? YES NO Circle one step in the music and label as **step**.

7. Can you find a **skip** in the measure? YES NO Circle one skip in the music and label as **skip**.

8. If the measure has a **melody**, describe how it moves.

UP   DOWN   UP AND DOWN   REPEATED NOTES

9. Look through the entire piece for marks that show **dynamics**. Write what you find below.

WP350

BEYOND THE PAGE

OBJECTIVES
• To apply theory concepts to music the student is learning and performing.
• To analyze the student's music for high/low, step/skip, melody shape, dynamics.
• To reinforce notation of clefs, notes, and time signatures.

TEACHING TIPS
• Give assignments for similar additional analysis (Music Investigation Report) based on the student's repertoire.

EXTEND
• Make your own Music Investigation Report to discover melody shapes that move only by step or only by skip in your music.
• Choose a page of your music and draw a dynamic color path you find.

EXCEL
• In the music you are learning, locate parts of melodies that look like "broken" triads on C, F, and G or other notes your teacher may suggest. "Broken" triads use the same notes of a triad, but are written one note at a time as a melody.

Example: C Major broken triad:

• Can you find a page of your music that does not have dynamics written in? Ask your teacher if you may create a dynamic color path for it (with pencil) on your music.

WP357

LESSON 14
MUSIC DICTIONARY

OBJECTIVE
• To review and use some of the symbols included in the Music Dictionary.

TEACHING TIP
• Encourage the development of good study habits by having students fill in page numbers as indicated in the right column.

USING MUSIC SYMBOLS

OBJECTIVES
• To use the symbols included in the Music Dictionary.
• To review symbols and terms used in EXPLORATIONS IN MUSIC, Book 1.

TEACHING TIPS
• An excellent way to review symbols and terms from the Music Dictionary is to have a group project where students make their own flash cards, with a symbol or term on one side and it's name or definition on the back.

EXTEND
• Create a matching game of your own using the terms from the Music Dictionary. Share it with other students.

EXCEL
• List terms and symbols that you discovered in EXPLORE sections of EXPLORATIONS IN MUSIC to expand the Music Dictionary.

48

LESSON 14 — MUSIC DICTIONARY

Watch the **MUSIC DICTIONARY** grow as you progress in the **EXPLORATIONS IN MUSIC, Books 1-7.**

Word	Symbol	Definition	First Found on Page (You fill in.)
ACCENT	>	A louder or stronger note or beat	24
ACCOMPANIMENT		A musical background added to a melody.	38
BAR LINE		Lines separating measures of music.	14
BASS CLEF	𝄢	A symbol drawn around the line F on the staff that shows notes low in pitch.	6
BASS STAFF	𝄢	The staff that shows notes from Middle C and lower.	6
CRESCENDO		To gradually get louder	41
DECRESCENDO		To gradually get softer	41
DOTTED HALF NOTE	𝅗𝅥.	The note that = 3 beats in 3/4 and 4/4	17
DOUBLE BAR		Used at the end of music. It is sometimes called "ending bar."	14
FORTE	*f*	Loud	41
GRAND STAFF		The treble staff and bass staff drawn together.	7
HALF NOTE	𝅗𝅥	The note that = 2 beats in 3/4 and 4/4	15
MEASURE		A section of the staff separated by bar lines and containing notes in groups of beats depending on the time signature.	14
MELODY		A line of musical notes moving up or down that can be sung or played.	32
PIANO	*p*	Soft	41
QUARTER NOTE	♩	The note that = 1 beat in 3/4 and 4/4	14
QUARTER REST	𝄽	The rest that = 1 beat in 3/4 and 4/4	18

WP350

49

SKIP		Moving from one note skipping over the next on the staff-from line to line or space to space.	32
STAFF		A group of 5 lines and 4 spaces on which music is written.	4
STEP		Moving from one note to the very next on the staff - from line to space or space to line.	32
TIME SIGNATURE	3/4 4/4	Shows how many beats are in each measure (top number) and what type of note = 1 beat (bottom number)	20
TREBLE CLEF	𝄞	A symbol drawn around the line G on the staff that shows notes high in pitch.	6
TREBLE STAFF	𝄞	The staff that shows notes from Middle C and higher.	6
TRIAD		Three notes that are written as skips apart.	36
WHOLE NOTE	𝅝	The note that = 4 beats in 3/4 and 4/4	18

USING MUSIC SYMBOLS

Draw a line from the symbol to its correct definition below:

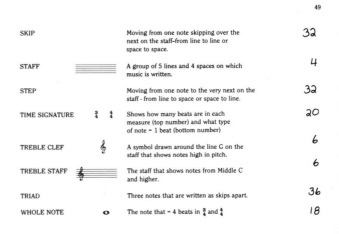

- separates measures
- shows high notes
- equals 3 beats in 3/4
- shows low notes
- ends the music
- equals 4 beats in 3/4 4/4

51

FINAL TEST

____ Your Score

TEST YOUR SKILLS

1. Write the **letter names** of the notes below. ____ of 8 points

A   E   E   C   B   D   F   F

D   A   F   A   C   C   B   G

2. Add **bar lines** and a **double bar** to the following examples. **Write in the counts** below each measure. ____ of 8 points

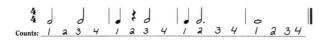

Counts: 1 2 3 1 2 3 1 2 3 1 2 3

3. Fill in each measure with **one note** that will complete the measure. Look carefully at the **time signature** and **write in the counts** below each measure. ____ of 8 points

Counts: 1 2 3 4 1 2 3 4 1 2 3 4 1 2 3 4

4. Write the counts below each measure. Then place the correct **time signature** in the box. ____ of 9 points

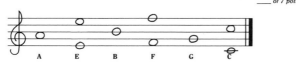

Counts: 1 2 3 4 1 2 3 4 1 2 3 4 1 2 3 4

52

5. Match the terms to the correct symbol. Circle the words and symbols that **do not** have partners. ____ of 5 points

A. half note   F   𝄞

B. quarter rest   H   ⎯⎯

C. forte   G   3/4

D. whole note   I   𝄢

E. piano   E   *p*

F. treble clef   A   ♩

G. time signature   B   𝄽

H. crescendo   C   *f*

I. bass clef   J   ⎯⎯

J. decrescendo   D   𝅝

6. Draw a **treble clef** on the staff below. Draw the notes that match the letter names given. ____ of 7 points

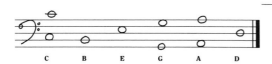

A   E   B   F   G   C

7. Draw a **bass clef** on the staff below. Draw the notes that match the letter names given. ____ of 7 points

C   B   E   G   A   D

Use the staff paper on page 50 for review of TEST YOUR SKILLS—Final Test.

TEST YOUR SKILLS Final Test

TEACHING TIPS

C clef: Number 1: Substitute C clef for either treble or bass clef. Answers (using alto clef) for treble substitution: B F F E C E G G; for bass substitution: C G E G B B A F. Numbers 6, 7, 8, 9, 10: Substitute C clef for either treble or bass clef.

Scoring Key:	POINTS	TOTAL POINTS
1. Each letter	1/2	8
2. Each bar line/double bar	1	8
Each measure of counts	1	
3. Each measure of notes	1	8
Each measure of counts	1	
4. Each measure of counts	1	9
Time signature	5	
5. Each correct match	1/2	5
6. Each note	1	7
Treble clef	1	

There are many details to check for the clefs! Any notes that match the letters given are correct.

7. Each note	1	7
Bass clef	1	

8. Melody written as described   5   5
The melody given as an answer is only one example. Any melody going up by step is correct.

9. Melody written as described   5   5
Melody on the answer sheet is only one example—any melody going up and down by skip is correct.

10. Each triad   1   6

11. Each measure of notes   1   8
    Each measure of counts   1

Explore Bonus:
    Each measure   1   2

8. Draw a **melody shape** on the staff below that moves up by step.   ___ of 5 points

9. Draw a **melody shape** on the staff below that moves **up and down by skip**.   ___ of 5 points

10. Draw the following **triads**.   ___ of 6 points

C MAJOR   F MAJOR   G MAJOR

C MAJOR   F MAJOR   G MAJOR

11. Fill in the measures below with the notes you have learned. Be careful to look at the **time signature**.
   Write in the counts below each measure.   ___ of 8 points

$\frac{3}{4}$ | || $\frac{4}{4}$ | ||

Counts: _____   _____

EXPLORE BONUS Write one of your rhythms from number 11 on the two-line rhythm staff.   ___ + 2 points

CLAP _____

STAMP _____

WP350

---

12. Each answer   1   6

13. A. Each answer   1   4

    B. Each answer   1   3

    C. Each answer   1   4

Answers for Listening Examples are on page 62 of the Student Book. Check that students are not referring to this page during the test.

54

12. Find the following in the example below. Put the correct letter name in the boxes.
   Note: Some boxes will be empty when you are finished.   ___ of 6 points

   A. dotted half note   D. double bar
   B. bar line   E. quarter note
   C. time signature   F. treble clef

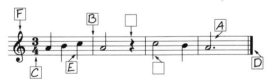

13. Listen carefully to the **EXPLORATIONS** tape!

   A. Are the notes you hear **high** or **low**? Circle what you hear.   ___ of 4 points

   1. (HIGH) LOW   3. HIGH (LOW)
   2. HIGH (LOW)   4. (HIGH) LOW

   B. Listen to the following rhythms. Is each one the **same** or **different** from the one written below?
      Circle what you hear.   ___ of 3 points

   $\frac{3}{4}$ ♩ ♩ ♩ | ♩ ♩ || (SAME)   DIFFERENT

   $\frac{4}{4}$ ♩ ♩ ♩ | ♩ ♩ || (SAME)   DIFFERENT

   $\frac{3}{4}$ ♩ ♩ | ♩. || SAME   (DIFFERENT)

   C. Listen to the following melodies that are moving **up**, **down**, or **up and down**. Circle what you hear.   ___ of 4 points

   1. UP   (DOWN)   UP & DOWN
   2. UP   DOWN   (UP & DOWN)
   3. (UP)   DOWN   UP & DOWN
   4. UP   (DOWN)   UP & DOWN

WP350

55

D. Identify the melodies you hear by filling in the letter names on the blanks.

1. Do you hear A or B? *B* ___ of 3 points

A.

B.

2. Do you hear C or D? *C*

C.

D.

3. Do you hear E or F? *E*

E.

F.

E. You will hear three notes moving by **step** or **skip**. Circle what you hear. ___ of 4 points

1. (STEP)   SKIP   3.   STEP   (SKIP)

2. (STEP)   SKIP   4.   STEP   (SKIP)

EXPLORE BONUS You can take a **listening challenge** and **write what you hear** for rhythm and melody.

1. **Rhythm:** Listen to the rhythm on the tape and try to **write** what you hear. The time signature and first note are given. Only ♩ and 𝅗𝅥 will be used. It will be played two times. ___ of + 4 points

23

2. **Melody:** Listen to the **melody shape** played on the tape and try to **write** it below. The starting note is written. Use only noteheads ● . It will be played two times. ___ of + 4 points

CONGRATULATIONS for learning so much! Turn the page if you want to **listen** and **explore** more!
WP350

56

EXTEND YOUR LISTENING

If you enjoyed the **EXPLORE BONUS** examples in **TEST YOUR SKILLS**, you may like to try a few more listening examples **writing what you hear**. ♩ ♩ ♩ and 𝅝 are used.

1. Listen to the following rhythm examples on the **EXPLORATIONS** tape and **write what you hear**. The first note is written. Each rhythm will be played two times. ♩ ♩ ♩. and 𝅝 are used.

24

1.

2.

3.

2. Listen to the following **melody shapes** on the **EXPLORATIONS** tape and **write what you hear**. The first notes are written. Use only noteheads ● . Each melody shape will be played two times.

1.

2.

3.

WP350

13. D. Each correct answer   1   3

   E. Each correct answer   1   4

Explore Bonus:
  1. Each measure   2   4

  E. Each measure   2   4

TOTAL TEST SCORE: 100 points
TOTAL BONUS SCORE: 10 points

EXTEND YOUR LISTENING

OBJECTIVES
• To reinforce perceptive listening for rhythms and melodies.
• To combine rhythmic and melodic notation with listening skills.
• To nurture inner listening by retaining rhythms and melodies in order to write them.

TEACHING TIPS
• This listening bonus could be called "the icing on the cake" in terms of total understanding of the concepts presented in EXPLORATIONS IN MUSIC, Book 1. Rhythmic and melodic dictation requires understanding note values, time signatures, movement up and down on the staff by step and skip, and the ability to write notes on the staff.
• Monitor the students as they listen to 🎵 24 and stop the tape after each example to allow students to hear the rhythms and melodies internally before they write. You will be able to identify students who are having problems and those who excel quite easily.
• Follow-up lessons can include more examples of separate melodic and rhythmic dictation for EXTEND activities and combined rhythmic and melodic dictation for EXCEL activities.

EXTEND
• Try additional examples of rhythmic and melodic dictation played by your teacher.
• Have friends notate rhythm and melodies you create.

EXCEL
• Try dictation combining melody and rhythm played by your teacher or another performer.
   1. Write the rhythm of the melody above the staff
   2. Write open noteheads on the staff to match the melody shape.
   3. Fit the rhythm to the melody shape.
   4. Draw bar lines to match the time signature.
• Create melodies with rhythms that can be used for combined dictation.

EXPLORE AND EXCEL
OBJECTIVES
These pages offer opportunities for students to experiment with the ideas they have learned in EXPLORATIONS IN MUSIC, Book 1. Do encourage them to fill the pages with imaginative ideas!

Page 59 offers space for an additional music story.

ANSWERS FOR LISTENING EXAMPLES
This answer page is located in the back of each student book for ease in checking ear-training examples. It is helpful for parents who assist with assignments and for older students who are more independent.

EXPLORE AND EXCEL

WP350

Write your music story below, using the manuscript paper to write the notes on the staff that spell your music words. Put in blanks for letter names under each note. Let your friends try to write the letter names of **your** music story! Draw a picture above your story.

Title: _____

By: _____ Date: _____

WP350

ANSWERS FOR LISTENING EXAMPLES

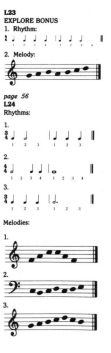

page 7
L1
1. A. Treble Staff
   B. Grand Staff
   C. Bass Staff

EXPLORE BONUS
   A. Violin
   B. Harpsichord
   C. Trombone

page 24
L11
1. A. SAME
   B. DIFFERENT
   C. DIFFERENT
   D. SAME

3. A. $\frac{4}{4}$
   B. $\frac{3}{4}$
   C. $\frac{4}{4}$
   D. $\frac{3}{4}$

page 34
L14
1. A
2. D
3. E
4. A. STEP
   B. SKIP
   C. SKIP
   D. STEP

page 44
L18
1. A. LOW and SOFT
   B. HIGH and SOFT
   C. HIGH and LOUD

page 45
L19
A. UP
B. UP & DOWN
C. DOWN
D. UP & DOWN

page 45
L20
A. STEP moving UP
B. SKIP moving UP & DOWN
C. STEP moving DOWN

pages 54 & 55
L22
A. 1. HIGH
   2. LOW
   3. LOW
   4. HIGH

B. 1. SAME
   2. SAME
   3. DIFFERENT

C. 1. DOWN
   2. UP & DOWN
   3. UP
   4. DOWN

D. 1. B
   2. C
   3. E

E. 1. STEP
   2. STEP
   3. SKIP
   4. SKIP

L23
EXPLORE BONUS
1. Rhythm:

2. Melody:

page 56
L24
Rhythms:

1.

2.

3.

Melodies:

1.

2.

3.

WP350

A DAY OF DYNAMICS

There are loud and soft sounds all around you! Explore " A Day of Dynamics" by listing the sounds you hear that match the dynamic colors you have learned. Listen carefully for sounds that you may never have noticed before!

>	f	p	<
decrescendo	*forte*	*piano*	*crescendo*
gradually getting softer	loud	soft	gradually getting louder

I heard the sound of:	Draw a dynamic color path that matches what you hear.

I heard these **very loud** and **very soft** sounds:

VERY LOUD	VERY SOFT

Explore: What are the music symbols and names for <u>very</u> loud and <u>very</u> soft? Investigate a music dictionary or ask a musician!

VERY LOUD Symbol: _____ Name: _____

VERY SOFT Symbol: _____ Name: _____

A FANTASY SOUND STORY

Imagine telling a story with motions and sounds but no words! Use your imagination to create a story that uses colorful sounds of all the dynamics below.

pp	*p*	*f*	*ff*	$\nearrow$	$\searrow$
very soft	soft	loud	very loud	gradually getting louder	gradually getting softer

1. Begin by writing some story ideas below. Choose a story that will be full of fantasy and colorful sound effects and perhaps some musical sounds as well.

Story ideas:

_____

_____

_____

_____

_____

2. List sounds you will use in your story and the dynamic sign that matches them.

Sound	Dynamic	Sound	Dynamic
_____	_____	_____	_____
_____	_____	_____	_____
_____	_____	_____	_____
_____	_____	_____	_____

3. Draw the dynamic color path that will match your story.

4. Now put all your ideas together by creating "A Fantasy Sound Story." Use motions to act out your story and sounds to create dynamic colors. Write out the motions and sounds of your story on a separate piece of paper. Now you can rehearse the actions in your story, using helpers to create sounds if needed. Perform your story for others!

Bravo! A job well done!

HIGH & LOW   LOUD & SOFT

1. Learn to listen to the world around you with finely-tuned ears! Music is often played in many of the places listed below and we often don't even listen to it. Be a music detective and record the dynamic level of the music you hear.

I heard music in a that was	Very soft *pp*	Soft *p*	Loud *f*	Very loud *ff*
TV commercial				
TV cartoon				
Supermarket				
Elevator				
Restaurant				
Clothing store				
Toy store				
Church/Synagogue				

2. What animals make **high** sounds?_____

What animals make **low** sounds?_____

3. List other **high** and **low** sounds you hear in everyday life.

High sounds I hear   **Low sounds I hear**

_____   _____

_____   _____

_____   _____

_____   _____

_____   _____

4. Choose one of the sounds from this page that you found interesting. Why was it interesting?

_____

_____

_____

_____

MUSIC IMPROVISATION

1. Explore the following combinations of **high and low** and **loud and soft** on your instrument. Write the pictures, moods, or ideas you think of as you "play with" (improvise) these sounds on your instrument.

Play	This reminds me of
The highest note you can play *f* :	
The lowest note you can play *p* :	
Three high notes moving down by step *pp* (very soft):	
Three low notes moving up by skip *ff* (very loud):	
Five high notes moving up by step *f* :	
Five low notes moving down by step *p* :	

2. Now that you have explored these different sounds, create a musical story with words and music **improvised** on your instrument. You can use the ideas from above as a starting point for your **music improvisation story.** Write story ideas below, expand your ideas to another piece of paper, and perform it for others! Have fun creating musical sounds and moods!

Title_____

Written and improvised by _____ Date_____

_____

_____

_____

_____

_____

_____

_____

_____